November 12, 2005

Peace and special blessings, Joann, for good health and happiness all during this coming year.

+ Fr. Jim Hennegree

Women For Women
St. Mary's Cathedral
Gaylord, MI

Sowing Seeds from the Gospels

Christian Homilies for the Liturgical Year B

by
James L. Menapace

authorHOUSE™

1663 LIBERTY DRIVE, SUITE 200
BLOOMINGTON, INDIANA 47403
(800) 839-8640
WWW.AUTHORHOUSE.COM

Table of Contents

Introduction

It is a typical cold, blustery day in Michigan's Upper Peninsula and it is the first week of Lent. The wind is blowing snow into soft, white drifts and you can feel the cold just by gazing out the window. The cedar, fir and pine are all shrouded in white and seem to be in a deep sleep. From all appearances they are dormant. But that is not so because there is much activity. This is the season of root growth and preparation for the warm spring rains. All of creation has its seasons. Winter will change into spring and suddenly spring will burst forth in new life. That is why in this Northern Hemisphere we celebrate the Paschal Mysteries with a deeper appreciation of our new life in Christ. It is the long winter of soul searching and then finding our roots grow deeper as we strive to live the Gospel message of love. The challenge we face as Christians is ever present in all the seasons of our lives. It is an endless task but let us begin. Our God is with us!

"In youth, because I could not be a singer,
I did not even try to write a song;
I set no little trees along the roadside,
Because I knew their growth would take so long.

But now from wisdom that the years have brought me,

I know that it may be a blessed thing

To plant a tree for someone else to water,

Or make a song for someone else to sing."

(Author unknown – From Barclay; The Gospel of Mark)

Hopefully my first attempt at publishing has been of some growth and value for those who read *Sowing Seeds from the Gospels Year A.* It is with the encouragement of many of my former parishioners, friends and family that these homilies for the Liturgical Year B find their way into print. Writing for me has always been a humbling experience and most of what I have written has probably been said many times over. Through that repetition I am optimistic that the Holy Spirit will inspire more reflection for those who are searching and longing for a closer union with the Lord of Life!

To write one must read and I am grateful for so many who have touched my life and renewed my faith, hope and love. Here are some of those great authors, the same ones you know and love: Henri Nouwen, Anthony De Mello, and Edward Hays, Joseph Cardinal Bernardin, Joan Chittister, Richard Rohr, Andrew Greeley, Walter Burghardt, Raymond E. Brown, Hans Kung, John D. Crossan,

Donald B. Cozzens, Matthew Fox, Bruce Chilton, William Barclay, Thomas Moore, Lewis B. Smedes, Sam Keen, and recently Marcos Borg.

I must also mention some of the homiletic services I have used over the years and they are: Celebration, Gold Label Publications, Markings, and 23rd Publications.

Finally I wish to express my gratitude to Ms. Mary Nelli who edited and proof read all of my homilies both for this publication and for the year A. She has been most helpful, inspiring and encouraging me in this ministry. I with to thank Ms. Winifred Blake and Ms. Eris Webb for their efforts in marketing my first publication and their insistence to do another series. I am grateful for my family and friends who now know an "author" and affirmed me in so many ways. Finally I value the staff at Author House publishing for their patience and assistance in the production of this book.

Seul Choix, Gulliver Lake

February 15, 2005

Francis of Assisi

PRAYER OF ST. FRANCIS

LORD, make me an instrument of your peace.

Where there is hatred...let me sow love.

Where there is injury...pardon.

Where there is discord...unity.

Where there is doubt...faith.

Where there is error...truth.

Where there is despair....hope.

Where there is sadness...joy.

Where there is darkness...light.

O Divine Master, grant that I may not so much seek,

To be consoled ...as to console.

To be understood...as to understand.

To be loved...as to love.

For

It is in giving... that we receive

It is in pardoning, that we are pardoned.

It is in dying...that we are born to eternal life.

The Gospel of Mark During The Liturgical B Cycle:

The following material regarding St. Mark's gospel is taken from William Barclay's Commentary. "When we study the Gospel according to Saint Mark,' declares Dr. Barclay, "we study the most important book in the New Testament, for in it we have the first life of Jesus ever to be written," the one on which all other accounts are based.

It is interesting to note that Mark is the earliest of the Gospel writers and that Matthew and Luke follow Mark's order of events. These three authors of the Gospels are referred to as the synoptic (from the Greek meaning "with the same eye") writers. From what we know, Mark is a nephew of Barnabas who traveled with Paul on his many missionary journeys even to Rome.

Mark's source of information probably was from the early Christian community that gathered in Jerusalem soon after Jesus' death. His basic source as far as we know is from Peter who was an eye witness of the Christ event. Most scholars would date Mark's Gospel about the year 65. Mark 16:9-20 is an addition and was added much later both because manuscripts were lost and the Gospel did not seem to be complete. It certainly is not Mark's style or language.

Some characteristics of Mark's Gospel: First of all Mark's aim was to give a picture of Jesus as He was known; Mark's Jesus is also the Son of God; God among humanity; He also emphasizes Jesus' humanity throughout his writings; Mark's stories have striking details of Jesus' life like no other Gospel; and finally Mark's Gospel is "the essential Gospel" being the first recording of Jesus' life.

Some suggestions for your reflection:

a) Prayerfully read the scriptures of the Sunday a couple of times.

b) Read the homily and take some time for reflection.

c) Share your reflections with others and share your ideas.

d) Finally prepare your own homily or thoughts for presentation.

1st Advent B

Scripture: Isaiah 63:16b-17, 19b; 64:2b-7, 1 Corinthians 1:3-9, Mark 13:33-37

It is true: all things sooner or later come to an end. We sometimes rejoice in that fact. But with each ending there is always a new beginning. It seems as though our lives are made up of endless change. We begin a new season in the church year, the season of Advent, a time of longing and searching, of watching and waiting, a time of expectation. We know that the Lord of life has come. Two thousand years ago He was born in a stable in a little town called Bethlehem. We know that He will come again; at the end of time, certainly on the day of our death. With faith we know that He is with us, everyday, every moment no matter where we go or what we do. He is truly Emmanuel, God with us.

The scriptures on this Advent weekend challenge us to be alert, awake and watchful. The Lord will come to us at a time we least expect. His coming is not to be a threatening or dreadful experience. No, on the contrary, we willingly and lovingly face the end of time in order to live more fully in the present. We do this not only to be more aware of our own spiritual needs and growth but also to take notice of all of our brothers and sisters who are also in need.

In the Gospel story the master leaves home and he places his servants in charge. That means we are responsible for our own preparation to make straight the ways of the Lord. We cannot delegate our spiritual welfare to others. Just as the Son of God freely chose to enter into our human history so we are challenged to follow in His ways. It will not be easy because to follow the Lord of Life demands the very best in us. There are no halfway measures here. No, those who freely choose his ways can expect to suffer, to have trials and difficulties of all kinds. There is to be a dying to selfishness and sin each day of our journey. However, we are not to lose heart in our struggles as we let go and let God be God for us.

That is why Paul assures us that God is intimately caught up in our human history. He has begun a good work in each of us and He will see it brought to completion. Our God is a faithful God. We lack no spiritual gifts as we await the revelation of the Lord Jesus in our lives. And not only that: We are to keep in mind that God is the potter and we are the clay. We are the work of His hands. All of us are in fellowship with the Lord Jesus.

Advent is the season to embrace all those things that hasten the approach of the Kingdom. It is a time to let go of everything that keeps God distant or outside of our daily lives. We are to be watchful, awake and on guard for His coming for the Lord has come to save us.

And so you may ask: What are we to do? Here is some practical advice. First of all enjoy this short and busy season. Welcome God into the world again by renewing His presence in your heart and in your home. Secondly, look for the signs of His love from your family and friends. Look into the faces about you and really take notice of the children and all those in need of your care, concern and love. It is in their faces that you will discover the God we all wait for and long to meet. Finally, know and realize, (make real) that God is present in every person you meet.

The Lord's coming in glory is not the end of the world. It is the world's new beginning. It is our task as followers of the Lord of life to be part of that beginning. God Bless!

2nd Advent B

Scripture: Isaiah 40:1-5, 9-11, 2 Peter 3:8-14, Mark 1:1-8

All of the scriptures on this second week of Advent bring us the comfort and assurance that our God is with us. He comes with power. Like a shepherd He takes care of His flock. He proclaims peace to His people. In the Lord's eyes one day is as a thousand years and a thousand years are as one day. The Lord does not delay in keeping His promises. We are to be people of hope. While waiting for His final coming we are to make every effort to be free of sin and at peace in His sight. We are to prepare a straight path. Every valley shall be filled and every mountain and hill shall be made low.

It is John the Baptist who also calls us to reform our lives, to make some changes in the way we live. Sometimes I think those changes that God would ask of us are not only a matter of selfishness and sin but also a change in attitude, a change in the way we look at life. Maybe this story can best explain what I mean. It goes like this:

"A man found an eagle's egg and put it in the nest of a backyard hen. The eaglet hatched with the brood of chicks and grew up with them. All his life the eagle did what the backyard chickens did, thinking he was a backyard chicken. He scratched the earth for worms and insects. He clucked and cackled. And he would thrash his wings and fly a few feet into the air like the chickens. After all, that is how a chicken is supposed to fly, isn't it?

Years passed and the eagle grew very old. One day he saw a magnificent bird far above him in the cloudless sky. It floated in a graceful majesty among the powerful winds with scarcely a beat of its strong golden wings. The old eagle looked up in awe. Who is that? He asked his neighbor. That is the eagle, the king of the birds said his friend. But don't give it another thought. You and I are different from him. So the eagle never gave it another thought. He died thinking he was a backyard chicken."

That can happen when we forget that we were created in the image and likeness of our God; that God Himself became like one of us in all things except sin. That can happen when we do not take time to know who we are. That can happen when we forget the promise that God is always with us, never against us. That can happen when people lose vision and hope and life becomes meaningless and filled with discouragement and despair. That can happen because of the troubled world in which we live, the hopelessness that comes because we don't know what will happen next and we feel helpless to do anything about it.

Hope is not a wish or even a dream. It is not even something you hope for. Hope is a virtue, a power, and a gift from God. It is a habit, a mindset, and an attitude by which we trust our God with our lives expecting only the best. God's gift of hope is a longing for certainty already ours. Hope is a future that has been around for a long time. This hope, Paul writes, will not leave us disappointed because the love of God has been poured out in our hearts by the Holy Spirit who has been given to us.

That is what this season of Advent is all about. We are God's chosen ones, a holy people, having dignity as sons and daughters of a loving Father. We are to fly with the eagles instead of "chickening" out.

Yes, you and I are to be people of hope, people of promise that our lives will end well and all of God's purpose in creating you and me will be fulfilled. What more can we ask of a loving Father?

As people of hope we are to remind others that they too can soar to the greatest heights, that life does have meaning and purpose, that every person has dignity and all of mankind will see the salvation of our God. We prepare the way of the Lord by telling good news, bringing peace to our troubled world, healing to those who are hurting, good example to those who have lost their way. We make those paths straight by sharing what we have with those who are less fortunate, forgiving and forgetting, seeking reconciliation with family and friends. The way of the Lord will demand the very best in us. And the very best is all that we can hope for. God Bless!

3rd Advent B

Scripture: Isaiah 61:1-2a, 10-11.
1Thessalonians 5:16-24, John 1:6-8,19-28

Our Advent is to be a time of waiting and watching, a time of longing but also expectation, a time of waiting by the window. We long for the day when we will have our lives in order and are able to settle down and really enjoy all that life has to offer. It is no easy task to know who we are and what we are called to be.

Remember, when we were young we thought it would all fall into place by the time we became twenty. Twenty came and maybe, just maybe, by the thirties it would happen. No, life begins at forty we were told and that wasn't the magical age either. Now we are almost sixty. To be honest most of us would have to say we are still in process, still becoming and it is going to take a lifetime. It is a good thing that our God is a patient God who has all kinds of time and will wait patiently for our response each and every day.

During this Advent weekend we again meet John the Baptist. He had his life all sorted out and people from miles around flocked to hear what he had to say. They had to find out who he was and what he was all about. John was not at a loss for words when it came to answering: "Tell us who you are so that we can give some answer to those who sent us." "No, I am not the Messiah. No, I am not Elijah, nor even the expected prophet. I am a voice crying out in the desert. Make straight the way of the Lord. There is one coming after me, the strap of whose sandal I am not worthy to unfasten." John was telling them he had found something, someone bigger than himself. John had found his God and he knew what God expected of him. He realized his call that he had a job to do and he was restless until it was done. That is the secret of life, the way to happiness, the purpose and goal of our faith. Someone once said: If we don't find something worth dying for, we will never find anything worth living for. How true that is. We are to find our God. Listen to His call, know our mission in life and then do it. It sounds so simple but it is no easy task. It demands the very best in each of us every day of our lives.

No, John was not the Messiah but he was a strong voice crying out and getting a lot of attention. He was not the light but he was a witness to that light. He was not the center of it all but he knew his place in the plan God had for the salvation of his people. Each of us in our own unique way has been called to the work of the kingdom. Each of us has special gifts and talents, that no one else has and they have been given to help bring that kingdom to fruition. When we fail to use our time, talent and treasure, we only prolong and delay that day when the kingdom will become a reality.

John knew what he had to be about because he was a man of prayer. Paul also reminds us this day that we are to never cease praying. We are not to stifle the Spirit given to us. We are to do good and avoid evil. It is our prayer that tells us who we are, and what we are to do. It is our prayer that gives us courage and strength to respond to the call that God has given to you and to me.

Isaiah would once again remind us and we need to be reminded often. The Spirit of the Lord is upon us. We have also been anointed, set apart to bring glad tidings to the poor, healing to the broken hearted, freedom to those bound by doubt and despair, release to those imprisoned by alienation and rejection. Isn't that what Advent is all about?

You and I are to announce a year of favor from the Lord to all those who have lost their way and no longer worship with us. We are to bring His peace to our troubled and violent world. We are to be people of hope, rejoicing in the Lord for He has called us to be his very own. He has given us a mission and He will be with us as we bring about His kingdom. You and I are a sign and promise of His love.

God Bless!

4th Advent B

Scripture: 2 Samuel 7:1-5, 8b-12, 14a, 16, Romans 16:25-27, Luke 1:26-38

Our lives are filled with all kinds of surprises. Most of the time they catch us unaware and off guard. They really open up our eyes to something new, something wonderful, something exciting. Sometimes surprises are frightening and we are afraid of what might happen next. There are other times, too when we just are not sure what God is doing, what He expects of us or how we will ever get the job done. For my ways are not your ways nor your ways my ways says the Lord.

Throughout the long course of human history, God has been acting in strange and unexpected ways, at a most inopportune moment, in a place not well known with a people who were not well liked nor appreciated. In a most astonishing way he prepares a dwelling place for His son. When Israel is under Roman domination, in a little town of Nazareth, Joseph of the house of David is betrothed to a young virgin whose name is Mary. "Rejoice O highly favored", the angel told her. "Behold, you will conceive in your womb and bear a son and you shall name Him Jesus". She is deeply troubled and scared to death. She wonders how this marvelous event shall come about. "Do not be afraid Mary, you have found favor with God and don't forget, nothing is impossible with God." And Mary said her yes. Let it be. Let it be. Mary's yes has changed the history of our world, never ever again to be the same.

By her Yes, the humble virgin of Nazareth made the gift of herself back to her God, a sign of her trust, her faith in His promises. When you stop to think about it: most of us when we pray beg that Thy will be changed, not thy will be done. No, I think I have a better idea of what should happen. Maybe we don't say it in those words but we try to twist God's arm. We try to have things go our way because we need to be in control, to be sure that we will live as the story books tell us: Happily ever after. It is not easy to let go, to let God be God, to trust Him when things don't go our way. We need a deeper faith in His love and a firmer hope in His promises. We need to be like Mary who was humble, obedient and poor, not poor in the sense of money or clothes or food but poor in the sense of total dependence upon our God, acknowledging Him as Our Father. Only those who are in need and recognize that they are not able to satisfy that need are free to be without fear. They are the ones who can rejoice in the God of surprises.

Remember nothing is impossible with our God. The one who was faithful to His promise to Mary is also the same God who invites us to bear His Son into our fragile and broken lives. Through that same Spirit that overshadowed our sister Mary, we can make Christ flesh again in our troubled world, during these difficult and sometimes frightening days in our lives.

What has happened two thousand years ago happens again this day. We need to surprise our God. Like Mary, we say our yes. Let it be. Let it be. That is a matter of trust and a measure of our faith. God Bless!

Let this be a sign to you: In a manger you will find an infant wrapped in swaddling clothes

Christmas

Who could have imagined that a peasant maiden would give birth to the Son of God? Who would have dreamed that a stable housed the King of Kings? Who would have thought that shepherds would welcome the Lord of Hosts? But that is how our God usually comes to us; through ordinary people in ordinary ways.

Like little children we are amazed. Our minds and hearts are filled with the wonder of it all. We need to express our joy and thanksgiving as we try to understand this mystery: God becomes like us in all things taking on our human nature so that you and I might become like God. What an exchange! This is the reason for our coming together in celebration this glorious evening.

We never grow tired of hearing about the world's greatest love story. It is all about angels and shepherds, kings and wisemen, heavenly choirs and lowly people, a young mother and a husband who find no room at the inn. It is all because of a baby born in a stable, a place where all creation shares in life. It is to those lowly shepherds that this homeless child brings the promise of a new tomorrow. That is why we find this story so fascinating.

Mary is overwhelmed with love. This father is overwhelmed with hope. This child will be someone very special. This child will be strong, wise and loving. These new parents of old are like all parents who have a special place by the manger.

Look at all those who come to worship at the crib: Many mothers and fathers have brought their children here, to this place to have them baptized. They, too, were overwhelmed with joy, full of hope, anxious to know what their son or daughter will become. They bring to this manger this evening their gifts of hard work, tiredness and hope for their children's future.

I see the faces of the mothers and fathers of our world where there is war and violence. Some fear for the safety and well-being of their newborn children. Others mourn their deaths. To this manger they bring their gifts of grief and worry, anger and fear and a promise of a new tomorrow.

Now here come the seniors, older men and women to the manger. They find the ground uneven and hard to walk on. Their eyesight isn't what it used to be. Arthritis has stiffened their joints. They too bring their gifts, the courage, the faith, hope and the love they have shown in the midst of so many headaches and heartaches. Their scars tell of their victories. They bring their loneliness and isolation, their sorrow and suffering.

Now the shepherds have come from the fields. Yes, they are the lowly ones. The angels have frightened them but their fears have diminished because they have seen the child. They bring to the manger the gifts of their work, their hopes and dreams for success, their anxiety about what tomorrow will bring. Along with all of their sheep they also bring those other shepherds they work with.

Behind them are all the workers of the world who share the same hopes and dreams, the same anxieties about the future. With them are the unemployed, the under employed, those who have no skills, all those dependent on the goodness of others or welfare. They bring their gifts, too, gifts of discouragement and poverty, their gifts of perseverance and hope.

And now through the streets of Bethlehem comes a huge crowd of people: All those who took to the streets and went in the market place of our mixed up world proclaiming truth, seeking justice, working for peace. They are the ones who marched for the homeless, the unborn, for equal rights and stood for human dignity and love. They have come to the manger to place their gifts of sacrifice, care, concern and love for others.

Each visitor to the manger reaches out to touch the child to receive a gift in return. In that brief moment they know that things will be different. This child will touch many with a love beyond all telling for all people, of all ages, and all times to come.

In the gift is the giver and in that gift giving the giver says: "I love you." The one who receives the gift is filled with joy and thanksgiving and says to the giver; "I love you, too." God has given us the greatest gift of all, the gift of His Son. In that giving He says to you and to me; I love you. In our joy and thanksgiving we exclaim to our God. I love you, too.

Come let us go quietly and gently to bear this gift to others. We will never be the same. We have met Jesus, the Lord of life. God Bless.

Holy Family

Scripture: Genesis 15:1-6; 21:1-3, Colossians 3:12-21, Luke 2:22-40

We may think that the little family at Nazareth had no real problems or struggles. After all, Jesus was the perfect son, never unruly, nor disobedient, certainly not spoiled like so many children of our day. Mary ran a perfect home, always neat, clean and tidy, no matter what was going on or who might visit. Joseph came in from his shop after a busy day to find a peaceful and tranquil setting with no worries, nor cares. But all of this is so far from their real life. The holy family at Nazareth was subjected to all the stress, tension and anxiety that are common in any family. They had the same difficulties of growth that all families must pass through. However, in that home where there was a great deal of love, Jesus grew in grace, age and wisdom as the scriptures remind us.

As we gather again in celebration all of our readings speak to us about family values and responsibilities. Fathers and mothers are reminded of their responsibilities to their children; children to their parents, husbands and wives to each other. We know that our families are the basic unit of our Church, our society and our world. If our families are faith-filled, strong and healthy, sharing care, concern and love, so will be our society and the world in which we live. If families have lost their way and their values, ignored the wisdom of the ages, then we can expect more divorce and separation, more violence and child abuse, more drinking and drugs, more of the same vicious cycle that our modern society suffers and experiences. There must be a return to the ideals of family life, where love reigns supreme if we are to find the happiness and peace we so desperately long for. We need the wisdom and insight of Simeon who saw the saving power of God working in and through this holy family. We need an appreciation like Anna who realized that God's saving work is centered in a family. It is in the context of the family that the Word is made flesh that God becomes man, that life has its beginning, is nourished and finds its fulfillment. A family is the place where love can truly happen.

To live together demands a great deal of giving in and sacrifice. Paul tells us what we are to do if we are to live well together. He says: Clothe yourselves in mercy, kindness, humility, meekness, patience and forgiveness. Above all we must love one another, which is not just a matter of words but also a matter of deeds. These essential family virtues don't happen just over night. We have to work at them every day. Families are to spend time together sharing all their hopes and dreams. Parents are to listen and not just nag their children. Children are to be respectful and obedient. And above all, they are to worship and pray together. The family that prays together stays together is an old saying. And there is more. There will always be more. The family is to be the source of healing and forgiveness for one another. If we do not find forgiveness there, where shall we ever experience it?

Your family is more than just a family. Your home is more than a place where you live. Children are a gift from God and parents are to teach them how to love. Your family is to be a sign of God's saving work for all of His people. That great work begins again today as we celebrate this feast of the Holy Family.

May your family grow in grace, age and wisdom each and every day of this New Year! God Bless.

The Magi

Scripture: Isaiah 60:1-6, Ephesians 3:2-3a, 5-6, Matthew 2:1-12

The story of the Magi finding the Child Jesus once again reminds us of the joy and happiness that should be ours during these days as we begin another New Year. This feast day helps us to become more aware of the wonderful gift of God who brings salvation to all peoples. In a real sense the holidays have not ended. They have only just begun. The Father's love for each of us is an ongoing call for the rebirth of His Son in our hearts and in our lives everyday of this New Year.

Like the wisemen, we too are on a journey. A New Year begins and we continue our search for the fullness of life, which is promised to each of us in the birth of Christ. Jesus is the light that shatters all darkness, all doubt, and any confusion and certainly gives us a sense of who we are and what we are called to be.

All of us search for meaning and purpose in our lives. We look for something or someone who can lead us on to greater and better things. We begin a New Year with a longing hope that things will be better, that the future will bring the satisfaction and happiness our hearts long for. There always seems to be something more, something beyond that next hill or that next turn in the road that will complete and fulfill all of our dreams. We are all restless. It is only God that can satisfy the longings of the human heart. We are to place all of our hope and trust in Him. We are to be like the Magi who were not afraid. They left family and friends, home and work and all their familiar surroundings to journey over hills and mountains, cross desert lands, struggling against cold and dark nights in pursuit of a star which they firmly believed would guide them to a new King.

The main point of the story of the three wisemen is that Jesus came for all, rich or poor, young or old, Jew or Gentile, white or black, male or female, slave or free. No one is to be excluded. He is a gift from the Father to all peoples of all times for you and for me and for all the generations yet to come. But there is also another point. Jesus came for those who are willing to search, for those who will not quit or give up, for all those who seek Him no matter how weary, disheartened or how frustrated life may become. Our search for Him is life long. It is endless and our hearts are restless until we rest in Him. It is a new time, another new year and we can make those changes necessary to be those beautiful persons God has called us to be.

Everyday our God challenges us to become something more than what we are. In our search we struggle against the forces of evil so as to grow to become God's holy people. The call is one of transformation. Our love of our God, our love of our neighbor and our love of self is the gold, frankincense and myrrh we bring. These new days will offer each of us many opportunities for growth as we continue our search.

With millions of people all over this world, we have been celebrating the birth of a baby, but our celebration is much more than that. With all the wisemen and wisewomen of two thousand years we rejoice and celebrate the victory of life over death, of light over darkness, of the coming of spring over the cold of winter, of hope over despair, of love over hatred, of peace and justice over violence and greed. On our journey through life, we follow a star, the Lord of life and He will lead us home to our Father for He is the Way, the Truth and the Life. God bless.

Baptism

Scripture: Isaiah 42:1-4, 6-7, Acts 10:34-38, Mark 1:7-11

S ome eighty miles south of a little town called Nazareth a great spiritual renewal was in progress. A humble man whose name was John was preaching repentance. He told his followers that the long awaited Messiah was coming. Huge throngs of people gathered to hear what he had to say. Many responded to his word and many were baptized in the Jordan River.

The day came when Jesus Himself appeared on the banks of that river and presented Himself for baptism. He waited His turn and then like all the others walked into the muddy waters of the Jordan and was baptized by John. The scenario is hard for us to understand: Jesus standing in line? Jesus, the Lord of life being baptized with sinners? Jesus being baptized by John? What does it all mean? Why did Jesus subject Himself to such a ritual?

I don't suppose we will ever know all the answers and be completely satisfied. But His baptism represents and expresses His yes as He freely accepts the work of salvation given to Him by the Father. As the scriptures remind us again this Son of God was also saying that He was the Son of man. Jesus is one of us, like us in all things but sin. He had identified Himself with those He had come to serve and save. He never set Himself apart from our human condition, the pain, suffering and anxiety that life has to offer to all of us. His mission began that day at the Jordan River and will conclude on a hill outside the holy city Jerusalem as He gives His life as a ransom for many, for you and for me.

It is through His baptism that Jesus identified Himself with our humanity. And it is through our own personal baptism that we identify ourselves with the Christ. We become one with Him saying yes to our Father. However, we know we have to say our yes over and over again. Our baptism is the beginning of a process of conversion that lasts for a life time. It is a day in and day out experience of change, transformation that leads from my will, doing it my way and at my convenience or pleasure to doing God's will in His time and His way, responding to His love.

Being anointed with the Holy Spirit and having His power we too are to go about doing good works and healing all who are in need. We do not sit in idleness, wringing our hands, wondering what we are to do next. No, we use the power given us by the Spirit to bring peace and justice to our tired and troubled world.

We are not to be a smoldering wick but a light that shatters the darkness of selfishness and sin. We are to open the eyes of those who are blinded by doubt, confusion and despair and don't know where to turn next. We are to comfort those who are bruised by the worries and cares of every day life. We are to help those held captive by their poverty, their lack of food or employment. Yes, you and I are called to change by our care, concern and love for our neighbor.

We must never forget that we are God's chosen ones, the favored sons and daughters whom He has called to a baptism of repentance. The biblical meaning of that word repentance is not beating up on ourselves for all our past mistakes and sinfulness but has the notion of seeing something new, a whole new way of living. It is doing something different than what we are presently doing.

Someone once said there are only three kinds of people in our world: those who make things happen, those who watch things happen and those who stand around and wonder: What happened? God bless

2ⁿᵈ OT B – View Sunday

Scripture: 1 Samuel 3:3b-10,19, 1Corinthians 6:13c-15a, 17-20, John 1:35-42

"Now what are you looking for?" Jesus asked. "Rabbi, where do you stay?" He answered them, "Come and see." So they just had to find out more. They went to see where He lodged and they stayed with Him the rest of the day. It is really unfortunate that we do not know what they talked about. We know that their time together was very special, very enlightening and very informative because they became His followers. One was Andrew, Simon Peter's brother and we are not sure who the other was, although scholars suggest it is John, the writer of the story.

Do you wonder what Jesus told them? Was it His philosophy of life? Was it about God the Father and the care that He has for all of His people? Was it all about salvation and life everlasting? What was it?

Maybe it went something like this. Maybe Jesus just talked about the broad view of life and what it was all about, that God is in charge and no matter what, He will take care of us. For every evil there is always a good. You can expect to find roses among the thorns, saints along with sinners. In fact, you will always notice that where there is sin, God's grace also abounds. God's last word about life is love, not hate, and hope instead of despair, faith instead of doubt and mistrust.

Maybe He also told them about the long view that God has about living. All things take time; good things come to those who wait. Victory comes out of defeat. Growth comes about through suffering and pain. Some things die so that others things might live. It is in giving that we receive. It is in pardoning that we are pardoned. It is in dying that we are born to eternal life. God knows that we have a long time, a long way to go to become fully human and He is prepared to wait for that day.

Maybe He told them what God really values. That God sees all things in a large way, the big picture and not only the little everyday common details of life. He sees all things in context. A headache is bad, Cancer is worse but hopelessness and hate are the worst of all. All things are judged by their goodness. We are judged by our hearts, our love. We are not judged by what we own or have or even by our success or our failure.

Perhaps these followers of Jesus were asked to take these same three views of life and make them their own. Maybe you and I should do the same.

First the broad view: We don't have all that we truly want, all the money, friends, and time we need. But we do have some of each. We should be thankful for what we have been given. We are to count our blessings each day.

Next, the long view: Things are not what they should be or even could be but one of these days things will come together and sooner or later we will find life is truly beautiful, great, worthwhile, fulfilling and enriching.

The value view: We need to get our values straight and not live as though life owes us a living. St. Francis was right. It is only in giving that we will receive. Being is more important than having. Good things happen when good people sacrifice and make them happen. People are always more important than things. Finally, God is the most important of all.

Now, whoever said that being a Christian is easy? It demands the very best in us. Every stage in life is a leap into the unknown. It is frightening and there is pain in change and growth. Remember what Cardinal Newman once said: "To live is to change and to become perfect is to have changed often." Most of us want life to be normal. We want all the answers and yet we prefer to keep things as they are; easy and comfortable. But that is not the way life is to be. The glory of life is that we are a pilgrim people, on our way to something more. One day we shall know the mystery we live but until then we must let go and let God be God for us because that is exactly what He wants to be.

Now I wonder if that is what Jesus and His disciples were talking about that day. God bless.

3rd OT B – Reform Sunday

Scripture: Jonah 3:1-5, 10, 1 Corinthians 7:29-31, Mark 1:14-20

Isn't it strange to think that the world as we know it is passing away? Heraclitus, an ancient Greek Philosopher said: "Everything flows and nothing remains." How true that is! Every day brings about change; something new, another challenge as we as a pilgrim people journey through life. Technology changes rather quickly. My new computer is already out of date. The economy changes; just look at the Dow Jones report each day. Governments change, the weather changes and we are hoping for some warmer days. Even our bodies change as we grow older. And most of us reserve the right to change our minds.

In the midst of all this change, Jesus announces that the reign of God is at hand. You and I are called to change, to reform our lives, to review our values and to consider what really matters.

Change for the people of Jesus' day began with the good news. They did not see God in terms of good news but rather as judge, jury and jailer. God was the avenger for sin. He would get even with those who did not live rightly and justly. When the people of Nineveh repented, God did not destroy them. They were given another chance. Jesus did not deny this fact but more often He thought and spoke of a God in terms of love. He taught those who flocked to hear His words that at the heart of the universe is a Divine Spirit who can best be understood as a loving Father. He taught His disciples to begin every prayer that way. In fact, He often referred to God as My Father and your Father.

Not only did Jesus teach this truth, He also lived it. Believing as He did He treated all people with dignity and respect. Children were very much a part of His world. Women felt safe and were appreciated in His presence, something that was unheard of in His day. The poor, the sick and all the social outcasts were welcomed with open arms. No one was excluded. Everyone was embraced in His love, rich or poor, young or old, saint or sinner. He had time and space for everyone. Since God loved all people, Jesus made that love evident. Yes, He not only preached good news, He also lived it.

Of course, this was a revelation to the people of His day and it fostered a revolution. How can this be true? The religious leaders refused to accept what He had to say. They knew very well knew how to deal with rebels and those who tried to change the system. It was a slow movement at first and it was rather simple, too. What harm would it do to talk about God's love and that they in turn were to love one another? However, if they really believed that, things could not continue as they were. There was something wrong with slavery, something wrong with oppression and tyranny, all that injustice that was so much a part of the world at that time. There is always something wrong with a system that refuses to recognize that each and every person has dignity and is valuable in God's sight.

From small beginnings great things happen. Look at those four fishermen who left their nets and father and followed after the Lord. Look at what they accomplished. They did more than change jobs. They bought what Jesus had to say and He changed them. They went on to continue His work and things have never been the same again. The biggest change took place in their hearts. They learned to love, to share their lives in care and concern for others instead of causing division and oppression. They learned how to give of their time, talent and treasure instead of taking and using other people for their own gain. They learned how to forgive instead of harboring all kinds of resentment and trying to get even. Resentment, some one said is like drinking poison hoping the other person will die.

All of us during this New Year are hoping for a better world, a happier life, and a more peaceful and loving family. If we want that better world and a better life and more loving family we have to work at it each day of our lives. It just doesn't happen over night. Jesus would once again remind you and me. Reform, change your lives and believe the good news. Anywhere, anytime, anyone does that the reign of God is at hand. God bless.

4th OT B – Spellbound Sunday

Scripture: Deuteronomy 18:15-20, 1 Corinthians 7:32-35, Mark 1:21-28

Some people are natural spellbinders. They grab our attention and we want to hear more. We are always in need of understanding others, ourselves and our world. We want to know what life is all about. We long to be fulfilled and made whole. We want to be healed of all of our worries, our suffering and pain, yes, all of our doubt and confusion. We long to put things together and find happiness and wholeness; which when you think about it, is another word for holiness.

This evening we hear how Jesus was also a spellbinder, how He held their attention. He was not like the Scribes and Pharisees. No, He taught with authority. He told them the truth and it is the truth that sets all of us free, free to make us truly God's holy people and that is what we are called to be. Jesus not only taught the truth but we say He is the truth. Jesus knows suffering and dying humanity. Since there was no way to know God, God came down to embrace our humanness, all of it. Yes, all of our joys and happiness and all of our suffering, pain, confusion and even death itself. All of life is now redeemed.

We all enjoy and take for granted the good days, the happy times, the vacations and the time we have off. But when you think about it, the times of suffering and darkness, of pain, sickness and even death are the occasions that shape, form and enable each of us to become real, whole and truly God's people. God is with us during those bad as well as the good times and we should never forget that. It isn't that He is the cause of our suffering or even desires that we suffer. We suffer because of our humanness, our selfishness and sin. We suffer because of our desire for power and control, for wealth and the easy life.

Our God is truly interested in eliminating all suffering. That is the point of the story about the man with the unclean spirit. Jesus not only preached the good news; he also lived that good news by healing that poor afflicted man.

The people of Jesus' day did not understand illness of mind or body as we do. They presumed those sick people were being attacked by an outside and evil force and they made that force real by calling it an unclean spirit, a devil. It is strange that some people still believe in a dualistic power in our world, that the devil or Satan is equal to God and goes about like a roaring lion ready to devour all in his path.

If there is a devil and I am not really convinced there is, that devil is in each of us especially as we selfishly think we can find the fullness of life on our own and in our own way. In this present time we may need to be exorcised of our need for things; hidden attitudes of buy, spend, invest and then work for more so that we can buy, spend and invest even more. We can be so caught up in this vicious cycle that we are driven more by our wants than our needs. As a consequence we miss the richness and most important joys of life.

We may need to be exorcised of our need and use of power. Who is it that said power corrupts and absolute power corrupts absolutely? Who has that power and how should that power be used in our modern world of getting ahead. Would the Lord of life approve of our use of power to climb the ladder of social success, business success to the detriment of the poor, the suffering and those less fortunate? Maybe the reason why so many families are unhappy is that there is an abusive use of force and fear in our homes when we should rather be people who love.

We may need to be exorcised because of our own personal selfishness, a "me first" attitude that makes all others second or sometimes last and that many times includes our God.

These may be just a few of the devils that possess so many and the sad part about it all is that they don't realize their plight. Once these "unclean spirits" are driven out, you and I are called to be healers as was the Lord of life. We just don't preach the good news; we try with all of our hearts to live it each and every day. God Bless

5th OT B – Job Sunday

Scripture: Job 7:1-4, 6-7, 1 Corinthians 9:16-19, 22-23, Mark 1:29-39

There have been times when all of us felt a bit like Job. We have had nights filled with darkness, all kinds of worry and fear, wondering what will happen next. Our days, too have their own kind of suffering and pain, difficulty and disappointments. Life is like the wind. We are here today and gone tomorrow. We wonder sometimes where to find our joy, our peace and our happiness. Everyone has days like that and our God truly understands our humanness and our search for wellness and a fulfilled life.

More and more we are beginning to realize that it really does not matter how long we live. It is really how well we live each day. Wellness is total well being, body, mind and spirit. It is more than just the absence of illness. It has to do with living life the very best we can each day, not waiting for something special to happen next week or even next month. It is truly becoming what God wants us to be. It looks toward our emotional, social, psychological and spiritual well being.

Jesus understands our need for healing in our daily lives. He came to cast out the powers of darkness and to rescue us for the kingdom of light. All of His miracles not only showed God's power over all evil but they were also a sign of God's care, concern and love for all that He has created. Did you notice that everyone was looking for Him? They sought His help because He was always concerned about the physical welfare of those in need.

He fed those who were hungry and satisfied the thirst of those who sought to know a new way of life. He taught the truth and then showed them by example how to love one another even those who did not agree with Him or opposed what He had to say. He opened their minds and hearts to realize that we are all God's people, His family created in His image and likeness. He showed us how to accept pain, suffering and even death turning all of those experiences into growth and new life. He was always there for the broken -hearted, binding up their wounds forgiving and healing those who in faith realized He had the words of everlasting life. Jesus, the Lord of life has come to bring the fullness of life to all who call upon His name.

To know and enjoy that wellness of life we are to be people of prayer. The scriptures often tell us that Jesus often spent time with

His Father. After a long and busy day, He got up early the next morning and went off to a lonely place and there He was absorbed in prayer. It was in prayer that Jesus found the spiritual and physical energy to go on to the neighboring villages to proclaim the good news there. He brought healing, wellness, to all who heard His words and followed in His ways.

You and I need to be prayerful people, but it is not just a matter of saying words. It is to know and appreciate God's love for us. When we pray we find our God within us and we are never alone, never overcome by the darkness, confusion, pain or suffering that all of us experience. We are refreshed and renewed to pick up our cross and follow in His ways. We find the necessary faith to let go and let God be God for us. Trusting in His love and His power, we know that all things work out for the good of those who love Him. For our God has the words of everlasting life.

At each Eucharist we celebrate, the Lord Jesus offers His saving life, death and Resurrection to the Father. We join in His sacrifice by offering ourselves, all of our joys and sufferings, all of our hopes and dreams, all of our pain and sacrifice, all that we are and hope to become. All of these gifts are transformed into a saving power for us, for one another and for our world. And that is the Good News

we are to share with all of God's creation. God bless

6th OT B – Leper Sunday

Scripture: Leviticus 13:1-2, 44-46,1 Corinthians 10:31—11:1, Mark 1:40-45

There is not anyone who likes to be left out or excluded. We don't want to feel like outsiders. Maybe you have felt like that at one time or another. When I first arrived here, I did not know what to expect. I wondered how I might be accepted, how I could find my way around, make friends and feel as though I belonged. It really took some time before I felt included. In high school, young people struggle to belong to the right group, to wear the right clothes, to be invited to the right parties. To be excluded is terrible. To be excluded is to be a failure at life.

Many people live everyday as outsiders, perhaps not because they choose to or even want to but it just happens to them. Single men and women, widows and widowers go home to empty and lonely apartments. Bag ladies and homeless men wander the streets of our large cities. Many have mental and emotional problems and don't know which way to turn. Feeling isolated from one another is one of the heaviest crosses to bear. That is why families are so important to every member especially these days when we spend so little time together.

The readings before the season of Lent speak to us about a terrible disease called leprosy. The Israelites forced the leper to live outside, away from family and friends. They had to wear torn and ragged clothes, shave their heads and cry out "unclean" as they made their way around. They not only felt the exclusion of others but also they felt that God also had cursed them with this terrible affliction because of their sinfulness. Because of that they even hated themselves. Even the Creator despised His creation. To whom could they turn for help?

It took a great deal of courage and determination for the leper to approach Jesus. Kneeling down he begged: If you will to do so, you can cure me. And so moved with pity, Jesus who had great compassion for this suffering brother stretched out His hand. "Yes, I do will it." He said. The leprosy left him then and there. An outsider was made to feel as though he belonged. Jesus touched the most untouchable of all people, a leper and he was cured.

Jesus, the Lord of life has touched our lives, too. He has forgiven us, every one of our sins and made us one family. We are no longer aliens, no longer strangers and outsiders but marked special as God's holy people. We are each sealed with His Holy Spirit. As Paul so often reminds us, we are all one in the Body of Christ, included in the Father's love. That is really the good news that we are to celebrate each and every day of our lives

Each day we are challenged to reach out and touch the untouchables in our society. We are to break down those barriers that separate us, those walls of pride, selfishness and fear so that no one is an outsider, nor ever feels alienated from God's care concern and love. We are to recognize that all people, no matter what color, creed or station in life are our brothers and sisters in the Lord.

The season of Lent will soon be here. It is our annual retreat. Now is the time to prepare and make some changes in the way we live out our days. We can begin this task by recognizing that we are all God's people in need of healing. Remember that a journey of a thousand miles begins with the first step, and we are never alone. The Lord of Life is always with us no matter where we go or what we do....God Bless

7ᵗʰ OT B – Yes Sunday

Scripture: Isaiah 43:18-19, 21-22,24b-25, 2 Corinthians 1:18-22, Mark 2:1-12

There is a word that we all love and it really is music to our ears. It is a simple word but one that is many times hard to say. You know what it is. It is only three letters long – y-e-s. Yes, I will be there. Yes, count on me for help. Yes of course, I will pledge to the PSA. Father Michael will like that. Yes, I love you. And there is more: Yes, go now in peace your sins are forgiven. Yes, take up your mat and walk you are no longer paralyzed. Yes, God is doing something new. He does love us; each and every one, saint or sinner, young or old, rich or poor. It makes no difference.

Ever since the beginning of time God has said His yes and all of creation has come into being, our beautiful world, all the oceans, the planets and stars, the sun and the moon. All that He said yes to, was good including all of His people. And to further prove His love He sent His only Son. And Mary, too said her word, yes, let it be, let it be. And that Word became flesh and dwelt among us. Jesus came and His life was a total yes to the Father: Yes, thy will be done.

This old world has never been the same again. He showed us how to say yes to the Father, not only in words, but also by his very life. This is the challenge that you and I face each and every day of our lives; to say yes to our God and really mean it.

Our God is trying to do something new for each of us and yet so often we are paralyzed in some mysterious way. Maybe it is fear, fear of what may happen if we say our yes to life and all that it has to offer. Walk down the streets of any of our towns and cities and you will notice many afflicted and paralyzed people. Look at the homeless, the wandering, alcoholics and addicts of all kinds. Many others are paralyzed by a dull drab, dreary routine of work, long hours, an unsatisfying job, fighting traffic morning and night. They can hardly wait for the weekend to come so that there may be a brief respite. Many of our young people and teenagers are bored to death with their gift of life paralyzed by a society and culture that does not know right from wrong, not knowing how to say yes or no. So many people are caught right in the middle and they never make a decision.

When you stop to think about it, all of us are somewhat afflicted in one way or another. Some are just paralyzed by their own greed, self-centeredness and pride. They never reach out to touch the lives of others. There are some who can never forgive, never forget. They dwell upon all kinds of paralyzing thoughts about others. Sad to say it happens in our families, with our co-workers, and sometimes with those we call our friends. Others are stuck in their old sinful ways and give up because they cannot forgive themselves for what they have done. They cannot understand how our God is compassionate, all forgiving, merciful and all loving.

That is exactly the point of this miracle story. We don't have to continue living as though we are not forgiven of all of our foolishness, all of our failures and sin. With God's help and grace we can be healed of our afflictions, pick up our mat and continue our walk through life. Paul is telling us that God has said His yes to you and me and that God always keeps His promises. That is hard to believe and like the scribes we might ask::" Who can forgive sins but God alone." The point really is that we can. Once we know we are a forgiven people we are able to forgive those who long for our forgiveness and love. That is what our yes to life is all about.

But there is more. When we say our yes it is not only said once and for all. Our yes is said over and over again each day to our God, to our wife or husband, to our children, to our families and all those we meet and love. Our God is doing something new each day and He is causing all that newness by our beautiful yes to life and to all its

goodness, beauty and love. Yes is a powerful and wonderful word.

God bless.

8th OT B – Love Sunday

Scripture: Hosea 2:16b, 17b, 21-22, 2 Corinthians 3:1b-6, Mark 2:18-22

S ome one once said that the Good News is too good to be true so many people don't believe it or even try to live it. They take a half-hearted approach to God's love and to life. I used to ask my students: What is the Good News? And they would answer: God is our Father, Jesus is our Brother and we are brothers and sisters in the Lord. Yes, we are all God's family. God loves us all. They knew all the right answers but they were not able to fully comprehend the implications of what they answered.

Several years ago there was a play on Broadway in which there was a conversation between God and Gideon. It went like this: Gideon says: God do you really love me? And God responds: Yes, Gideon I do. Gideon says: I don't understand why. God responds: To tell you the truth Gideon neither do I.

Yes, God's love is a mystery. God does love us; no ifs, ands, or buts. There are no conditions attached to that love. He has called us to life, not a dull, drab existence but the fullness of life each and every day. It is a life lived out in love.

The challenge you and I face is to respond to that love by loving God with our hearts, mind and soul, our very being and our neighbor as ourselves. How many times we have heard that preached and it seems to be accepted only in a half-hearted way.

All of our scriptures this evening speak to us about that difficulty. Hosea's story is all about the tender, caring, faithful love of our God lived out in the context of a marriage. Yet many still cling to the old fashioned notion of a God of rules and regulations seeing their faith only as obedience to a distant God who goes into a long pout and tries to get even when we fail to meet His expectations. The opposite is true for Hosea. He experiences God in an intimate way similar to a beautiful marriage and he responds to that love with trust and faithfulness.

Paul reassures the people of Corinth that they are signs of God's love. It is written in their hearts. Those who know and make Jesus, Lord of their lives show forth the love of God in no half-hearted way. Did you know that the personal stories of our individual lives become chapters in the larger story of salvation history? Many people who never darken a church door or open a bible may come to know the love of God only through your dedication and concern for their welfare and well-being.

There truly is something sad about those who accept the gift of life in a half-hearted fashion. It is like a marriage that is just going through the motions; a friendship without true concern and love for another, a group of players without a team effort. Jobs are lost or businesses disappear because there is little enthusiasm for the quality of work or dedication to service. I think we all lose respect for people who don't know what they believe in or what they want out of life. It seems if we have never found anything worth dying for, we will never find anything worth living for. It also seems that you have heard that before.

Jesus does not tell us we are to patch old garments with new cloth nor are we to put new wine into old wineskins. Something new is happening. We are to change our old worn out, threadbare ways of living life. What he encourages is whole heartedness in embracing His way of life; no compromises, no half way measures, no looking back but facing the future with hope, confidence and trust in Him. Whole-heartedness is the secret of success in all that we do. And there is much to be done.

Sowing Seeds from the Gospels

Here is one good example of what I mean. Two weeks ago Father Michael talked about the Annual Pastoral Services Appeal. He spoke about the needs of the diocese as well as those of the parish in furthering the mission. He rightly asked that each family in this large parish consider making a substantial pledge toward achieving the goals he outlined. When we stop to recognize and realize the many blessings and gifts given by our generous God, you and I have a responsibility to make a generous response. Stewardship can really be defined as a gratitude attitude. Have you expressed or will you express your gratitude in a sincere way? Are you truly grateful for all the many blessings, the gifts and talents the Lord has given to you and your family? Remember all that you have received is a gift because of His love for each and every one of us. God bless.

1st Lent B – Temptation Sunday

Scripture: Genesis 9:8-15, 1 Peter 3:18-22, Mark 1:12-15

We all look for the short cuts in life. We prefer to take the easy and fastest way out, the least demanding way to get something done. After all, we say, there is no point in re-inventing the wheel. This seems to be an unwritten law and we live by it each day. We seek pleasure and try with all of our might to avoid pain, suffering and sacrifice. Freud was really right, wasn't he? After a few experiences of life however, we soon learn there is no easy way out. Life will demand the very best in us and our God will be there to see that we do just that.

On this first weekend of Lent, we hear how the Spirit sent Jesus out into the desert. There in that wasteland of forty days the Lord was tested. A force drove Him there so that He might experience humanity in all of its weakness. Like you and me Jesus was tempted to take the easy way out and avoid the way of suffering and sacrifice. He was tempted to think that He could manage his life on his own, building an earthly kingdom rather than serving His Father and His kingdom. He was tempted in every way that you and I experience life, in discouragement, doubt and despair. Jesus knew temptation. He knows our human condition. As the scriptures so often remind us: He was human like you and I in all things but sin.

However, He also knew that His Father would be with Him at all times, in all circumstances, in all the events of His day. He knew His Father would be there to strengthen and encourage Him to make the right decisions, to help Him proclaim good news.

So often we think that we are weak when we are tempted but it is exactly the opposite. Our temptations come to strengthen us and give us an opportunity to do even greater things. Gold is always tested and purified in fire. If we are to be patient people, then we can expect to have many occasions to become impatient. Patience comes from a Latin word *"patior"* meaning to suffer and that is why they call people in the hospital "patients." There can be no virtue where there is no suffering.

If we are to be kind and loving in the things we say and do, then there will be all kinds of opportunities to be selfish, self -centered and concerned only with our own needs, forgetting the suffering and pain of others. If we want to be humble people, we can expect others will test our pride, maybe by finding fault and expecting us to act like they do. There can be no growth in virtue unless we are given a choice, unless we are tested to do the opposite.

In our day, I think that many of our temptations deal with attitudes, with doubt, discouragement, despair and depression and our disregard for others and their feelings. Many times we prefer to take the easy way out and just give up trying to do good, to really work at becoming the beautiful person God has called us to be. We go along with the crowd who suffer those same kinds of faults and failings that are common to each of us. The sad part is that we can become so comfortable with things as they are that we don't realize that things can be different, that our lives could be better.

Maybe that is why we have these forty days of Lent. Maybe we will recognize our need to make this world a better place for everyone and not just for self. Maybe Lent is just what the doctor ordered. What a wonderful opportunity for all of us. It seems if we have never found anything worth dying for, we will never find anything worth living for.

The Lord knows our weaknesses, our doubts and confusions, all of our temptations to take the easy way out. And in spite of all that He still loves us.

Temptations are a part of life and so is sin. The Lord knows our humanness. He forgives our sins and all of our failures to love as we should. Remember, our God is with us especially during these holy Lenten days as we strive to live out His Good News. God bless!

2nd Lent B – Glory Sunday

Scripture: Genesis 22:1-2, 9a,10-13,15-18, Romans 8:31b-34, Mark 9:2-10

Strange as it seems there are many people who have never had an experience of God in their lives. Maybe it is because they look at life as a problem to be solved rather than a mystery to be lived. Maybe they are so blasé about life, that they never get excited about the first signs of spring, the birth of a child or to see the beauty of someone who has fallen in love. Maybe they are just too busy getting ahead, making money and spending it. Maybe they are just too satisfied with things as they are and they do not want change of any kind. If we never take time to stop to smell the roses, we will never have an experience of God who loves us and takes care of us each and every day.

On this second weekend of Lent, we hear about the transfiguration of the Lord, a very significant part of His life. Jesus takes His friends, Peter, James and John up onto a high mountain. There He is transfigured before their eyes. It was a peak experience for them. They began to realize and accept what Jesus was all about, that He would suffer, die and rise on the third day. Peter for the first time was speechless. This is my beloved Son. Listen to Him. Now they knew; through suffering and death, through failure there is new life, the promise of salvation. Usually we think of Jesus' transfiguration as a triumph of glory but there is more, much more. Jesus accepted His ultimate failure, His death on a cross. For Him the two went hand in hand: first death and then glory.

When His family thought He had lost His mind, He found himself some new friends. When the hometown people rejected His words, He went off to other towns. When those people refused to accept what He said and who He was they turned Him over to the Romans to be crucified. He then went "home" to His Father. Jesus learned obedience from the things He suffered.

It would also be good for us if we learned obedience by accepting the hard facts of life from the things we suffer. It would be good if we learned to accept failure as a necessary part of life instead of being surprised by it or trying to find some easy solution for all of our suffering. But we will never come to terms with these lesser failures until we recognize and accept the failure of death.

All of us know that sooner or later we are going to die. But we pretend that it won't happen for a long time; maybe when I am eighty-three or so. We separate death from life itself. Yet every day we die a little and each year brings us closer to the grave. We are frightened of death and try to make something eternal. Love is forever we say and it is. But sometimes it isn't. Maybe it wasn't love after all. Maybe love just died.

We like to think that our children will comfort us in our old age, that they will carry on our name and all that we had worked for. And they should, but sometimes they don't. Maybe it is not their fault. It is because all of us are orphans and strangers born out of due time into a world of mystery.

Children like to think their parents are perfect. And they ought to be. But sometimes they are not. It is not because they don't want to be but just because no one is. Parents can fail their children. But when we bury our parents we also recognize their humanness along with their love and we decide to love them all the more.

All of us know that life is good, beautiful and precious. However, we need to also realize that life's failures are just as important as all of our successes. We are all losers as well as winners. But there is something sacred and timeless, something that never fails. It is our God. God takes all of our failures in hand and makes them whole. To experience and know His presence in our failures gives us the courage to go on.

You and I learn obedience from the things we suffer along the way. We live and learn how to die to our selfishness and sin and finally let go and leave the mystery of life to our loving God. That is exactly what Jesus' transfiguration is all about and that is how you and I are also transformed into the likeness of the one we profess to love. God Bless

3rd Lent B – Temple Sunday

Scripture: Exodus 20:1-17, 1 Corinthians 1:22-25, John 2:13-25

All of us are in business. Each day money is earned and money is spent. Each day we work, we sell ourselves, our gifts and talents, our time and all that we have to earn a salary or wage which we use to provide the essentials of life and maybe a few extras now and then. It is not easy to make ends meet these days especially with the high cost of living and our need to get ahead. Sometimes we seem to be in competition with one another. Still many of us have to watch our pennies and live within our budget.

The buyers and sellers in the temple area were also in business. They knew how to make a few shekels and even more, they knew how to take advantage of those who came from a distance to offer sacrifice and pay the temple tax. Jesus did not like what they were doing and He told them so, not only in words but also in actions, driving out the sheep and oxen and knocking over their money tables. He was angry and they knew it. What a shocking scene for so many! His Father's house was not to be a market place. Of course, they did not like it. On whose authority do you do these things? Who do you think you are? After all they had been paying their temple tax and worshipping God since the days of Moses. They did not understand that the worship of God was a lot more than external offerings of animals and a few shekels. Jesus tried to explain that to them, but they were unwilling to listen. The worship of His Father would not be in a temple or a building, nor was it a matter of animal sacrifice. Their worship had to be from the temple of their hearts.

I think there are some people who even today think they are in business with God, or that God is in business with them. Do this and do not do that. Keep all the rules and regulations of the Church. Earn your way to heaven by paying your temple tax of being here each Sunday and being a nice person. But you can not go through the motions and not be real about worship. Worship of our God is a day in a day out experience of God as our Father who calls us to a greater intimacy with Him and one another.

First of all God is not interested in our fasting, our works of charity or even our prayers if these good works do not lead us to a greater love for Him and for one another. God wants our hearts; all that we are. He wants our very lives and He will not settle for anything less.

Each of us is of the highest value in his sight. God has no favorite sons or daughters, nor are there any strings attached to His love. When you think about it, our lives are a gift. We belong to Him and His love for each of is everlasting. We have been forgiven over and over again. I think we need to hear that again and again until we realize that we are loved. Jesus knew that. It wasn't the temple that was profaned, or the Sabbath, or even the Scriptures. It was people. He was angry because a few greedy people were taking advantage of many needy people.

They had come to worship, to have an experience of God, to seek His forgiveness and love and they were not made welcome, nor were they helped in their need. Instead of doing good for others, those money grabbers were feathering their own nest, settling for a few shekels of ill-gotten gain. No wonder He was disturbed.

We are in business, all of us are. But it is our Father's business. It takes people secure in their faith who are willing to take risks and make sacrifices to feed the hungry, clothe the naked, to console the sick and suffering, to lift up the lonely and broken-hearted. The rewards for this kind of business are a rich and happy life here and the fullness of life hereafter.

Now, I wonder what the Lord would say about our presence here this day! God Bless.

4th Lent B – God's Gift

Scripture: 2 Chronicles 36:14-16, 19-23, Ephesians 2:4-10, John 3:14-21

Every so often someone in a crowd of people at a sporting event or on TV will raise up a sign that reads: John three fifteen. Have you ever wondered what that is all about? Why is that passage from scripture so important for so many people? I think it is because it speaks of God's love for each and everyone of us. And there is more. It is a love that is freely given, undeserved, a love that cannot be bought or earned in any way. There are no strings attached to God's love. It is a love that can only be accepted and joyfully received.

The gospel reading on this fourth weekend in Lent is from John three fifteen. It is part of a conversation that Jesus had with his friend Nicodemus. Nicodemus had come to Jesus to find out what the mystery of life was all about. Jesus told him and He also tells you and me that God so loved the world that He gave His only son that whoever believes in Him may not die but may have eternal life. He goes on to say that those who do not attain eternal life remain in darkness. But that darkness is not because they have not done enough to deserve the light but rather they have simply refused to accept the light and the life that God offers to all peoples in Jesus, the Lord of life.

I think that most of us believe that God freely loves us. But there are many that cannot accept or receive that love. For them the good news is too good to be true so they will not believe it. There has to be something going on. After all there is nothing free in this life. There must be some strings attached, some kind of gimmick. Many are always suspicious of things that come too easy.

Maybe it is because we are afraid of what we are getting into. It may cost us more than what we are willing to pay. Maybe it is because we feel that good things just don't happen to us unless we earn them by our good works. When we work hard for something, we say we have earned it. It belongs to us. We have a right to it and no one can take it away from us. Many times we like to think that we are in charge of our lives and that we alone are responsible for all the good things that we do.

And there is a third reason why many are afraid to accept God's love. We suspect that free gift of love because we don't deserve it. Deep in our hearts we have this strange feeling that we are not worthy of His love. We have failed so many times. We have done such terrible things. We have hurt so many people by our selfishness that we think that we are also unlovable. Maybe God has written us off and we are just not valuable.

Paul tells us very clearly in that second reading that all these reasons for not accepting God's love just don't make sense. He goes on to say that God does not think or act like we do. We are the objects of God's love simply because He has chosen to bring us to life. God loves us period! His love is a gift. God does not give to us because we have done anything to deserve His gift. They are not merit bonuses. Nor are God's gifts investments given in hope of a return. He does not trade. God just gives. God gives because He loves. Let no one take pride in accomplishments. All that we are, all that we have, all that we can become, all of it is God's love for us. It is a gift, freely given.

We give and are generous with our time, talent and treasure because God was generous with us first. God has given us the greatest gift of all, the gift of His Son. He waits for our response. If we give only to influence God to increase our wealth, we are not giving, we are investing. If we give to avoid suffering some punishment we think we deserve, then we give only as a bribe. We give because we love. We give in return because God has first given all things to us including our very lives. When we give with generosity and a heart of love, it reminds our neighbors, our friends and families and ourselves of God's everlasting love for all of creation. Now how will you respond to God's love this coming week? God bless

5th Lent B – Seed Sunday

Scripture: Jeremiah 31:31-34, Hebrews 5:7-9, John 12:20-33

Everyday God speaks to us in many ways. Sometimes we are so burdened by our worries and work, so busy with our lives that it takes a crash of thunder to get our attention. Then there are other times when we think that God's voice is like the whisper of angel wings. He comes to us in our quiet prayer and reflection to help us appreciate His care, concern and love. No matter how God is speaking in your life and in mine, it is most important that we listen and take to heart what God is saying.

This evening, on this fifth Sunday of Lent, we hear the Lord speak to us and His words are hard and difficult to accept. Jesus tells us: We must lose our lives in order to find them. If anyone would serve me, let him or her follow me. To follow in His way is to take up our cross each day. No one wants a cross. Most of us would rather choose the easier way to go. Who wants to suffer? Who wants to die? But strange as it seems Jesus is telling us that life comes through death. He is really saying that we are to die to all of our self-centeredness, our selfishness and sin in order to rise again to newness of life. It is only by struggling with our daily problems and difficulties that we find a better way to go. It is by facing worry, anxieties, frustration and fear that we grow in faith, confidence and courage and the hope of new tomorrow. Growing up, becoming wise, finding happiness, becoming whole and complete and holy can only be found by our constant and deliberate everyday efforts.

Sad to say most of us learn that the hard way; by our mistakes, our failures and defeat, our humiliation, pain and suffering which is very much a part of being human. That is the cross we are asked to bear. In the end, it is our final suffering of death that brings us to Resurrection and life everlasting.

When you think about it, all the trials and tribulations that come our way are really invitations to a greater life. Most however, see them as something to be avoided at all costs. We expect a pain free existence. Take two aspirins and it will all go away. Like the life locked up in a shell or husk of a seed, we can refuse to die. We can say no to a new way of life. We can refuse to change our comfortable, soft, easy and boring routines. Some are unwilling to take on any new responsibilities, never risk sharing their lives with another. They seldom speak of their hopes and dreams, never their failures and foolishness. Some never take time to encourage the young or bring comfort to the old. By saying never, we never enter into the fullness of life. We sell ourselves short of the life that could be ours. There is an old saying and perhaps you have heard it before but it is very true. "If we have never found anything worth dying for, we will never find anything worth living for". Maybe that is the problem so many people face in our busy, mixed up, tired, old world.

It seems that there are really only two kinds of people in our world: those who love life and those who just live it; those who are willing to give and those who only take, those who ask what's in it for me and those who ask: what can I do to help? There are people of faith who lovingly accept all that life has to offer and there are others who do things their own selfish way and find life unfair. They are filled with bitterness, criticism and complaint. They are part of our world and it is easy to tell them apart.

I think most of us will have to admit that there is no easy way out. There are no short cuts to the good life. Either we are on the way with the Lord of Life or we are in the way of His kingdom. Unless the grain of wheat falls to the earth and dies it remains just a grain of wheat. But if it dies, it yields an abundant harvest. Let everyone

heed what they hear. God Bless

PALM SUNDAY B

Scripture: Isaiah 50:4-7, Philippians 2:6-11, Mark 14:1 – 15:47

Once again we begin another Holy Week. It is like a three day mini-retreat and we do not want to miss any of it. It is the high feast days of our Church and these celebrations are special to millions of people all over our world. The liturgies of these beautiful days invite us to enter into the passion, the suffering, death and Resurrection of the Lord of Life. It is not an easy invitation to accept. We shun the cross, the sign of suffering, pain and death. We turn our face away from that shameful way to die and we wonder why: Why the cross? Great thinkers have been asking that question for years.

Wasn't there any easier way? Maybe Jesus could have avoided that death. He could have gone into hiding. He could have given in and told those in charge that they misunderstood Him. He could have been silent and just ignored their charges. The authorities would have welcomed a chance to ignore Him, even though He was a trouble maker. But Jesus would not allow it. No, Jesus freely and lovingly takes upon Himself a burden that He did not have to carry. He does so to prove to you and me that God loves us and cares for us in spite of all of our foolishness, failures and sin.

Jesus is put to death primarily because of the political issues of the day. He proclaimed a new way of living that was threatening to both the religious rulers, the Scribes and Pharisees as well as the Roman authorities. He spoke out very openly for the poor, starving and hungry people who had little to live on and no hope for their future, making life miserable and intolerable. He criticized those in authority who laid heavy burdens upon the shoulders of the feeble, the sick and the old. His hopes and dreams were to bring a freedom to all who were caught up in slavery of any kind, those who suffered injustice and prejudice, and those who were "the poor" of His day, and there were many. Jesus had no other way to go if their suffering was to be alleviated. He had come to bring everyone the fullness of life, not a dull, drab, dreary existence. And that is so for you and me this day.

Some how and in some beautiful way we, too, are caught up into the Paschal mystery of Jesus. In a sense we also go up to Jerusalem. We are called to stand firm in our faith in the face of suffering, pain and death when it is much easier, a lot safer and more comfortable to be silent, to hide or never take a stand on issues that make for a better life for all.

It takes faith, a great deal of hope and a lot of love to accept the palm branch we are holding because we know that branch leads to the tree, the tree of the cross. Down deep in our hearts, I think we realize that, for every year we take our palm branches home and place them behind the cross that hangs on our living room walls. It is an uncomfortable reminder of what we are called to be. We are challenged once again to respond in a Christ-like way to all the suffering, poor and downtrodden, all those neglected in our own neighborhoods, towns and cities.

This is a holy week and we are called to celebrate these three days in a special way. They will be a source of enrichment for our faith, hope and love even amidst our fear, doubt and confusion in these difficult and trying days. What do we celebrate you ask? We celebrate a love story that has no end. It continues on in your life and in mine. God Bless.

If I do not wash you
you can have no share
in my heritage

Some Holy Thursday Thoughts:

These celebrations are the great and high feast days of the Church year filled with all kinds of symbols and meaning for our faith. All of salvation is acted out for us in Word and Sacrament.

Awareness is most important! Why do we do the things we do? We often need reminders that God does love His people and that He is with us as we journey through these days of salvation. We also need to be reminded that we are not in business with God. God's love is always there and not dependent upon what we say or do or accomplish with our lives.

Tonight we celebrate the institution of the Eucharist, the Bread of Life, in the context of a meal shared with those we love. There is no way that we can eat a supper with those we dislike.

Something special takes place during this meal. Jesus washes the feet of His disciples. It is a humbling experience for Peter. He does not understand and does not want his feet washed. "You will never wash my feet Lord!" "Oh! Peter if I cannot wash your feet you cannot have any part with Me!" "Then Lord wash not only my feet but all of me." It is significant that the Lord is not interested in hygiene but rather holiness.

The Lord is concerned about internal dispositions rather than just external appearances which are primarily for show. People wash and clean, put on their Sunday best and then come to Church. But not much is changed internally. Our call is to get our heads and hearts together.

"If I as Lord and Master wash your feet then you in turn must wash others feet." To both give and also receive is an act of humility and many times the more difficult part is to receive than give.

The Eucharist is food for the journey of life which in turn gives us the courage, strength and love to humbly do our Christian work of loving others as we love ourselves. In other words, the Eucharist is not an end in itself but the means whereby we bring God's love into our troubled world.

We become Eucharist for others, signs of God's unconditional love. Isn't it rather strange that most of us have pictures of the last Supper in our homes and rarely do we have a picture of The Lord humbly washing the feet of His followers?

Good Friday

Yes, Jesus dies! What cruel and mean way to die! He was nailed naked to a cross. It all began about nine in the morning. They say He died about three in the afternoon. He was buried in a tomb not even his own. No greater love has anyone than to lay down his life for another.

This is Good Friday and many wonder why we call it good. It was a terrible, frightful, dark day of death. Many wonder who the greater fool is. Was it the one who was put to death or those who choose to follow in His ways rather than the ways of the world? Yet, we glory in the cross of Our Lord Jesus Christ who is our life and our salvation.

When we look at the cross, we are filled with all kinds of mixed feelings and emotions. We shudder at its sight. We turn our eyes away. We know that the cross asks too much of us. For it reminds us of our own death. It tells us that death is real. It is painful and a deep dark mystery. It is a reminder to all of that we shall die. Jesus died and I will die. My parents will die. My children will die. Everyone that I love is going to die. Those are hard and cruel words for a world that tries so hard to convince us that death does not exist, that we can stay eternally young. So what do we do? We pretend. We close our eyes and turn our back on all the suffering, all those who are sick and we avoid those who are terminally ill. We separate from our neighborhoods those who are mentally or emotionally ill or retarded. We hide the old and the wrinkled. We hear of death and there is no funeral. The body is quietly taken away and there is no time for mourning or healing comfort.

As we kiss that bent cross on this Good Friday, we face the greatest fear of all. Some day I will die. None of us will get out of this alive. We should know that because each of us experience separation and death many times as we journey through life. It is all those small and large sufferings we experience. It is injustice, hatred and revenge. It is the headaches and heartaches both physical and mental. It is broken homes and broken friendships. It is separation and divorce, all kinds of failure and foolishness. It is selfishness and sin.

But there is much more to that cross. We embrace it. We venerate it. We hang it up in our homes and wear it around our necks. For we see in that same cross victory, new life and Resurrection. That cross is also a sign of love. It tells us about the love of God who freely gives us His Son to be our Savior and Lord. It tells us about Jesus who lets go of His life so that you and I might live. It is also a sign of all those who freely give of themselves; lay down their lives for others; mothers and fathers, friends and neighbors, all the great women and men who have gone on before us. They make this old world of ours a better place for us to live. They give us a glimpse of what the kingdom is all about. For nothing ever gets changed, nothing worthwhile happens, nothing is ever finished unless we, too, are willing to sacrifice, to pay the price of loving others.

Good Friday is only one day but Easter is forever. And Paul goes on to say: "For what seems to be God's foolishness is wiser than men's wisdom and what seems to be God's weakness is stronger than man's strength." It is the paradox of the cross. God Bless.

*This is a night in which heavenly things are
united to those on Earth and things divine to
those which are human.
Alleluia-Alleleuia-Alleluia*

Easter Sunday B

Scripture: Acts 10; 34a, 37-43, Colossians 3:1-4, John 20:1-9

On this Easter morning I bring you grace and peace from God, Our Father, His Risen Son, Our Lord Jesus Christ and His Holy Spirit. May this celebration deepen your faith; renew your hope so that you may know His love for you and your loved ones. This is truly the day the Lord has made. Let us rejoice and be glad! This Man, Jesus, whom they nailed to a cross, is alive and well. He who died is now raised. What a surprise for His disciples! What good news for you and me! Our faith tells us there is a new day dawning, a new spring coming and we believe that to be true with all of our hearts.

The followers of Jesus and all His friends knew the joy of Easter only after the defeat of a Good Friday. They really thought He was dead, that they would never see Him again. All their hopes and dreams of a new age were shattered and buried with Him. The stone was rolled into place. The entrance of the tomb was closed. In their minds it was all over. It was the end of this Jesus of Nazareth with all His stories, all of his promises of a new way to live life. Yes, they were disheartened, discouraged and filled with despair. Who wouldn't be?

Then early in the morning, on the first day of the week, while it was still dark they had the greatest surprise of their lives. The stone had been rolled back and the tomb was empty! It was a situation that Mary could not face alone so she ran back to tell Peter and John what she had seen. They didn't understand what she was talking about so they had to go to see. Peter entered in amazement and wonder but John saw and believed. He was the first of many to understand and to believe. He experienced the Risen Lord! Love gave him eyes to read the signs and the faith to understand. It is only with love that we are able to grasp the truth and come to believe. No amount of rational proof can convince us of this unbelievable good news. The promise of Easter is that all who believe in Him will have everlasting life.

The events of that first Easter morning are believed by millions of people. They are believed most fervently even though the event itself was never witnessed. They have experienced the Risen Lord in their lives and He still lives on in all those who believe.

Whatever brings you here this day; your deep faith in the Risen Christ, the demands made upon you by your family or friends or that vague yearning down deep inside that something in Jesus' story has a lasting meaning. All are parts of God's greatest surprise in our lives.

There is more to the Easter story. The world must know about the goodness of our God, that God cares for all that has been created. The world must know about the value and dignity of each human life because God dwells in each of us. They must know that we believe in a God of life not death, a God of compassion and mercy, not a God who ignores pain and suffering, a God of forgiveness and not revenge, a God of peace not war, a God of love not hatred. They must know the Risen Lord in their lives, also. Who will tell them about our God if it is not you nor I? Our world is dying to hear some good news.

May these joyful days of Easter bring forth new hope and a new life for all of God's people. God Bless.

2nd Easter B – Thomas Sunday

Scripture: Acts 4:32-35, 1 John 5:1-6, John 20:19-31

Sometimes April is a strange month. It is a mixture of winter and spring and sometimes we are not sure what will happen next. It can be a violent month, thunder and lightning, plenty of rain and then surprisingly warm, sunny days. April is child birth month. The earth is in labor to be born again. April is Good Friday and it is also Easter Sunday. But we know in faith that a new day is dawning, a new spring is on its way with summer to follow. Because it always does, we know that it will happen just as day follows night.

Thomas had a hard time to accept the fact that life comes through death. He could not believe until he had seen the Risen Lord. And then he had to put his hand into His side: "My Lord and my God." He recognized the Lord as the same Jesus he had known and loved before. It was by that power of love that Thomas was moved to believe. It almost seems as though Jesus was scolding Thomas for his lack of faith. But that was not so. There are many ways to come to faith and doubting may be the only way for some people to find their God.

Faith is a life long process of exploration and discovery and sometimes that journey is filled with all kinds of detours and ways that seem unsure and unsafe. When it comes to faith I do not think that any one of us has it all together. We are always searching and looking for ways and means to make our faith stronger and deeper.

The scriptures on this first week after Easter remind us once again that our journey of faith is filled at times with doubt and darkness, failure and fear, locked doors and closed minds. Sometimes life can be filled with turmoil and confusion. It almost seems that we have less faith when it comes to living through a difficult period of disappointment, sickness or the death of a loved one. However, it is exactly at those times of trial that our faith is strengthened and renewed. It is then that we realize that Jesus has the words of everlasting life. Like Peter, we have to say: "Lord, to whom else can we go?"

When we talk about faith we should not make the mistake that we can sort things out by thinking up some good arguments or reasons to believe. We may be able to do part of it by reasoning but faith is a gift from God which also involves our trust, and that is a matter of the heart. It also includes our faithfulness in living out what we believe and finally it involves the promise of a new and hope-filled tomorrow. The kingdom of God is here and it is yet to come. All of this is a matter of faith.

The story of Thomas would remind us that faith without some struggle really isn't much faith after all. Even if our faith is as small as a mustard seed we have a good start and with that faith we can move mountains.

We know that spring follows winter; April does give way to May and summer breezes. We also know that the darkness of night turns into the brightness of day. Our God will bring Resurrection, new hope and new life to all those who follow in the way of His Son. Our only response after all is said and done is to proclaim good news to others by living out what we believe. God Bless.

3rd Easter B – Surprise Sunday

Scripture: Acts 3:13-15, 17-19, 1 John 2:1-5a, Luke 24:35-48

Life is filled with all kinds of challenges, changes and surprises. We wonder what is going to happen next. We prepare our agenda, set forth our plans, mark our calendars and hopefully wait for things to go our way. But life is not that structured. It is filled with surprises, unexpected events, joys and sorrows that color our days and change our lives. All of us would agree: Life is a mystery! Many of our greatest hopes and dreams never become real, but thank God most of our worries and fears never do either. God has a plan for each of us and it is filled with all kinds of unexpected events.

Those who followed the Lord and remembered Him in the breaking of the bread wondered what to expect next. Where would they go? What could they do? How would they ever pick up the pieces of their lives and start over again. Suddenly Jesus walked into their lives, quietly and calmly just as though nothing out of the ordinary had happened. "Peace be with you," He said. They could not believe their eyes. They certainly did not expect Him. It must be a ghost. But He does not look like one. "Don't be anxious or disturbed. Look at my hands and my feet. It is really I. Do you have something to eat?"

After eating with them He began to open up their minds and hearts to understand the scriptures. "Didn't you realize that the Messiah must suffer? Don't you understand that He would be put to death and then on the third day rise from the dead?" Little by little it began to make sense. They were able to look beyond their suffering, their loss and failure, even beyond the death of the Lord to find a new life, a new beginning, a Resurrection. Now they knew what was expected of them. They had come to a turning point in their lives, a point from which there would be no turning back. They knew the Risen Lord in their midst and now they would be witnesses, signs of His presence in the world. They would be believers but also doers of the words they had heard. They were transformed into a whole new way of seeing life.

As we celebrate these Easter mysteries, we, too, are to be witnesses of what we believe. If people are to believe in the Resurrection of Jesus they must see it in our lives. We begin this good work by reminding ourselves that we are loved, that we are a forgiven people and that loving forgiveness is to be shared with all those who have hurt us or have rejected or failed to love us.

This forgiveness must begin in our homes, in our families, in our place of work, in our neighborhoods, and our Church. We are to be God's unexpected love in the lives of others by our care, concern and willingness to forgive and forget serving their needs.

On that Easter evening the Lord of Life brought His peace to His disciples. He calmed all their fears and they knew His forgiveness. He ate with them and then opened their minds and hearts to receive His love. In this Eucharistic celebration the Risen Lord is also in our midst as we gather in His name. We share in the one bread and drink the one cup of salvation making ourselves one in His love. We experience His peace and then we go out those doors to bring that peace, forgiveness and love to others. We are witnesses of what we believe. God Bless

4ᵗʰ Easter B – Good Shepherd Sunday

Scripture: Acts 4:8-12, I John 3:1-2, John 10:11-18

Whenever we think of shepherds and sheep our minds drift off to some foreign land or some ancient times. We know very little about sheep and even less about shepherds. Today we proclaim Jesus to be our Good Shepherd. We say this Good Shepherd knows His sheep and they know Him. This Good Shepherd freely lays down His life for His Sheep. It is really hard for us to understand that kind of love.

Maybe this modern day love story will help us to appreciate our call to be good shepherds to one another. It could very well happen here at our Medical Care Facility. It goes like this: Like a judge handing over a sentence, the doctor gives his diagnosis to a female resident. "You have Alzheimer's disease." The patient appears confused. "What does this mean?" Next to her is her husband of forty years. One look at him and anyone would realize he knows exactly what this means. From the beautiful and strong, supportive and loving wife he has known for their many years together he will watch her become a dazed, drooling invalid who now stares past him with empty eyes. He watches and grieves. Many of their family and old acquaintances find it just too uncomfortable to be near her. But he remains at her side caring for her with all the love in the world. He holds her hand. He feeds her, changing soiled clothing throughout the day. When evening comes he helps her into bed and waits until it is dark and she falls asleep He does all this realizing that she will never be able to care for him again, that she will only get worse until that terrible day when she will not even know who he is. The story ends ten years later when he ties a bib around her neck and feeds her a piece of cake in celebration of their 50th wedding anniversary. The very next day she dies.

This is a love story of a modern day good shepherd who lays down his life for another. It is a story of someone who refuses to give up on another person no matter what. She was stripped of everything that we call human, everything that might attract others but he did not leave her side. He loved her until her last breath. He gave his life in loving service to the one he loved.

Our Good Shepherd asks us to be good shepherds to each other. We are to listen to His voice, not only as He speaks to us in prayer and scripture but also in the voices that are crying out for our care, concern and love. We are to search out those who have wandered away from the flock and need guidance and good example to find their way back home. We are to invite and encourage our young families who no longer worship with us and do not know Jesus as their Good Shepherd. We are to remind others who are hurting and walking through the valley of darkness that the Shepherd has concern for all of His flock, for all those in need of healing. We are to help others to listen to the voice of our Good Shepherd especially those who might become pastors in our parish churches.

The work of being a good shepherd begins in our homes, in our families where there sometimes is dissension, misunderstanding and an unwillingness to forgive and forget.

The closeness and intimacy we feel there in our homes will confirm that we are loved and that we will be able to share that love with others.

We are to remember that our Good Shepherd laid down His life for all of us and He did so only because He loves us. We express our thankfulness when we are good shepherds to all those who come to us in their need. Watch and be aware of some one this week who needs your love. God Bless.

I am the vine
you are the branches

5th Easter B – Vine Sunday

Scripture: Acts 9:26-31, 1 John 3:18-24, John 15:1-8

It really does not matter how long one lives, it is really how well one lives each day. All of us want to live the very best life possible, having good health, finding some peace and happiness along the way, being fulfilled and successful.

I read something from Emerson that he suggests is the successful life. Here it is: "To laugh often and love much, to win the respect of intelligent people and the affection of children, to earn the approval of honest citizens and endure the betrayal of false friends, to appreciate beauty, to find the best in others, to leave the world a little bit better whether by a healthy child, a garden patch or a redeemed social condition, to know that one life has breathed a little easier because you have lived." This is what it means to succeed.

All of us have one life to live and we hope and pray that it will be meaningful. Our scriptures on this Sunday give us some wise advice and insight into the successful life.

Jesus compared Himself and His followers to a grapevine. Within that vine there were two kinds of branches; those that bore fruit and those that were barren. The barren branches were cut away, gathered into piles and burned. The fruitful branches were pruned so that they would yield even a greater harvest.

As branches and part of that vine, you and I receive our life. Jesus is really saying that in some beautiful and mysterious way He lives in each of us and we are to find our daily life in Him. He alone is to be our strength, the source of all energy and power. The image of the vine and branches tell us that we are part of something much greater than self, that we belong to a family, a very large family, a group of people called the Church, the Body of Christ. It also says that you and I need others that we depend upon their care, concern and especially their love. Apart from this vine there can be no life, no chance to find real happiness, no peace, nor any success. In fact, without the Lord, we are like withered, rejected dry old branches ready to be burned.

And there is more. There will always be more. There is no room for just sitting pretty on that vine, resting thinking all is well. We are to give glory to Our Father by bearing much fruit. We are to love in deed and in truth and not merely talk about it. We are to love one another as He has commanded us to do. The barren branches on the vine were not evil. They did not bring forth bitter or even sour grapes. They were just useless branches, yielding no grapes at all.

It was Mother Theresa from Calcutta who said that we should do something beautiful for our God each and every day. It isn't that God needs that beauty; we need to be signs of that beauty by the proper use of all the special gifts and talents that we have been given to build up God's kingdom. The things we do, need not be grand or spectacular or beyond our abilities. The Lord will accept the smallest gift from a loving heart and turn it into the greatest and grandest successful life ever.

If Jesus is the vine and we are the branches then we are mostly intimately united to Him. Intimate is a wonderful word. It comes from the Latin which means to make myself known to another. We can only do this in prayer. Take time during this week to be intimate with the Lord and know that He will be intimate with you. God Bless

6th Easter B – Friendship Sunday

Scripture: Acts 10:25-26, 34-35, 44-48, 1 John 4:7-10, John 15:9-17

All of us know and sense loneliness at times in our lives. It is part of our human condition and experience. However, there seems to be an epidemic of loneliness and alienation these days. In our busy and hectic lives we seem to lack the friendship, the usual warm family and spiritual ties which would help eliminate much of what we experience. Loneliness is an emotion, a feeling and a fear of being alone. It is a five year old leaving home for the first time and not knowing anyone at school. It is growing up and no one seems to notice or even care. It is being chosen last because you are clumsy, awkward and stumble over your own feet. Loneliness is lying in a hospital bed, looking at the ceiling and asking: "Why, why me?" It is the loss of a loved one after thirty, forty or fifty years of being happily married. Loneliness is realizing that in some ways you can never go home again.

Jesus knew loneliness. He was human and it was also part of His life. He spent time in prayer knowing the Father's love for Him. He shared His life with some very close and intimate friends; Peter, James and John and with Mary, Martha and others. He told them: "As the Father loves me, so I also love you. Remain in my love". On the night before He died He also said that there is no greater love than this, to lay down one's life for another. Then He said something very special: "I no longer call you slaves, servants. I call you my friends". The way to deal with loneliness is friendship with our God, friendship with self and friendship with others.

First of all, Jesus is our friend. The promise He made to His friends in that Upper Room is the same promise He makes to you and me. "I call you friends since I have made known to you all that I have heard from My Father. It was not you who chose Me. No, it was I who chose you." As a friend Jesus will be with us always no matter what. His friendship and love is there in good times as well as bad, in sickness and health, in failure as well as success. Even when we turn away from Him, His love for us will be there. That love is the same love the father has for his prodigal son waiting for his return. That is the sign of God's friendship with each one of us.

Secondly, friendship with self. Without being a friend to self we cannot love others. We need to realize and appreciate that all of us are special, have dignity and are worthwhile in spite of all of our weaknesses, all of our foolishness and sin. We need to embrace the shadow in our lives, accept our humanness and strive again to become more patient, more gentle, more loving of self. We need to know that God loves us just as we are right now! He knew us from the very first moments in our mother's womb. The Hound of Heaven continues to pursue us down through the seasons and years of our lives until we meet Him face to face.

Finally, because love is of God, we are to be friends. Our love like God's love is to be all inclusive. No one is to be left out. God's love is an embrace of all that He has created. Strange as it seems in our need to be loved, we live more of our false self pretending that we are better than others, superior because of class, education, power and wealth. We live in a very competitive society. It is getting ahead no matter who or what stands in the way. Someone once said that there is so much selfishness and greed in our world that there is not enough to go around. Isn't that scary? Isn't that sad when people are so concerned about their own interests, taking care of their own selfish needs that they forget that we are all brothers and sisters in the Lord? To exclude others is to fail at friendship and loving. Why is it that separation, division and alienation and loneliness are the common words of our every day lives?

We heard that God shows no partiality. Everyone is acceptable to Him. We are to extend our friendship and love to others by sharing our time, talent and treasure. What really becomes good for you and me becomes the good of our neighbor as well. The Lord has called us to be friends. Like those early believers, we might be surprised at what can happen when the Holy Spirit opens our minds and hearts in friendship with others. God Bless.

Ascension B

Scripture: Acts 1:1-11, Ephesians 4:1-13, Mark 16:15-20

It was the twenty-sixth day of December 2004, the day after Christmas that our world was shattered and broken in two. It was the gigantic undersea earthquake and huge tsunami that took the lives of over two hundred thousand people. It left many other hundreds of thousands people homeless, helpless and hopeless. The stories were beyond telling and comprehension! The amazing part of this most terrible tragedy was the response made by nations, organizations and so many individuals. It was heartening and encouraging to see such a response and the tremendous outpouring of care, concern and love shown by everyone. We were all tightly bound together in a cause that makes this world a better place for the suffering, the poor, *the aniwim*, the little ones of God. We became more unified than ever before. Goodness, gratefulness and good news was made real in all of our lives. It is a tragedy like this that again reminds us how small our earth has become and our need to care for one another.

On this feast of the Ascension we hear Jesus tell His followers they are to continue the mission that He has entrusted to them. They are not to stand around, looking up at the sky, wondering what to do next once He is gone from their midst. They will have the necessary gifts, the strength, courage and power to do some wonderful things. He promised that His Spirit would be with them all days until the end of time. They had to trust in His promise if ever they would be able to bear witness to all He had told them.

Witness is a wonderful word if understood correctly for us as followers of the Lord. We can be present and witness an event like those reporters who told us about the tsunami tragedy. We can witness during a court trial or be present at a signing of a decree or law. The witness the scripture is referring to has to do with the personal knowledge of Jesus, the Lord of life. If we are to be witnesses of the Lord and His way of living, we need to give evidence of what we believe. That evidence can be observed and judged by what we say and do each day in our lives. Someone once said: "Who you are speaks so loudly that I cannot hear what you are saying!" The media is the message as we have heard so often. We preach more by who we are.

Paul said it in that second reading: "Brothers and sisters I urge you to live in a manner worthy of the call you have received." The key words he lists are humility and gentleness, with patience for one another and preserving the bond of peace. He goes on to say: "There is one Lord, one faith, one baptism, one God and Father of us all who is over all and through all and in all!" These are beautiful words to ponder and reflect upon. You and I are to be one in mind and heart to evidence and witness what we believe.

That does not mean that we are to be all the same. In fact, God has made us all different, unique and in that beautiful diversity each of us continues the ministry of the Lord. All of us have special gifts and talents to share. Some of us make our worship experience meaningful. Others are busy assisting the poor, hungry and homeless. Still others are teachers, doctors, nurses and social workers. All of us contribute to the mission of the Church in one way or another. We are the Church, the People of God as Vatican II called us. The Lord challenges us to proclaim good news in a world that longs for purpose, meaning and happiness.

We gave evidence and witness to what we believe by our sharing with the people who suffered the tragic events of the tsunami. That was a powerful one time experience for all of us. However, the ministry of Jesus continues every day and we are to be signs of His presence. Take some time this week to notice the needs of those around you. Be the evidence they need to believe the Good News. God bless.

Pentecost B – Spirit Sunday

Scripture: Acts 2:1-11, 1 Corinthians 12:3b-7, 12-13, John: 20:19-23

We live in an age of locked doors. We have keys to open and to close, to make our lives secure, to be sure our homes are safe and sound. We lock our cars, sometimes with the keys in them! We lock our cabins and even our Churches. We truly live in fear; fear of what can happen next, fear of the dark, fear of forced entry, even fear of one another. All those locks and alarms are meant to free us from fear, from worry, from our sleepless nights but they fail to do their job. Instead they cause us to isolate ourselves from the world and from one another. All of our locked and closed doors alienate us, cause disunity and disregard and generally make life miserable.

The followers of Jesus had locked the doors of that Upper Room because they were afraid of what would happen next. What if the powers in authority came looking for them next? Even though they tried to lock out the world, Jesus was able to enter and stand before them. "Peace be with you", He said. In other words don't be anxious; don't be afraid. It is really Me! "As the Father has sent Me so I send you. Receive the Holy Spirit." Then something wonderful happened! They were changed, transformed from fearful followers to fearless people fired up to do the Father's will. They became enthusiastic, a beautiful word (which is from the Greek meaning in God).They were inspired by the Spirit to live the good news. The Lord has given them His peace and the power to forgive. They changed their fearful ways and their world would never be the same again.

The gift of the Spirit is the power to forgive and forget. It is the gift of freedom, a wind blowing us toward a new creation, a new unity of purpose. The Spirit helps us to heal all separation and division and gives us a new hope for peace in our hearts, in our homes, in our neighborhoods and in our world.

The Lord Jesus comes to us with His peace, invading all of the upper rooms in which we try to lock ourselves away from others. He would have us turn our enemies, real or imagined, into allies and friends. Jesus comes to show us His wounds, His hands and side. They are not signs of defeat but of victory and triumph over all evil, sin and even death. He comes to give us His peace, a peace that the world cannot give.

Finally we hear in the gospel story the words of challenge. "As the Father has sent me, so I send you." Our task is to bring His peace to our troubled world. That is exactly why we need the Holy Spirit. It is the Holy Spirit who will guide and direct us in the ways of the kingdom.

All of us have received the power to forgive. It is not only the ordained that can loosen or bind. Each of us is called to forgiveness just as the Lord has forgiven us. We say this every day in our prayer: Forgive us our trespasses as we forgive others theirs. How can we expect forgiveness when we are unwilling to extend that same forgiveness to others? We begin first of all in our families where so often some members have not spoken to each other for the longest time. The next area of forgiveness is in our neighborhoods, in our schools and also at our place of work. If we choose not to forgive, we continue to lock ourselves up in our anger, suffer resentment, alienation and a lack of peace which we desire with all of our hearts. We are all in the need of forgiveness. We all make mistakes and often miss the mark. We are all cut out of the same cloth.

It is the Holy Spirit who will make us one because we were all baptized into one body even though each of us has different kinds of spiritual gifts. That is why we need the Holy Spirit to unite us in all

of our efforts to build the kingdom. Come Holy Spirit; fill the hearts

of your faithful and enkindle within us the fire of Your love!

God Bless.

Trinity B – Father's Love Sunday

Scripture: Deuteronomy 4:32-34, 39-40, Romans 8:14-17, Matthew 28:16-20

All of us have our own special and unique experience of God, our own personal faith. We can learn from others, from a mother or father, from our teachers and our friends. We can learn from reading and studying. But when it comes down to our faith in God it is our day to day experience that really counts. It is our prayers, and our problems, our wonders and wisdom, our doubts and despair, our faith and our hope and love that speak to us in our every day experiences. It is God who reveals Himself from moment to moment in all that life has to offer, in people, in events, the trials and tribulations that help us to grow, change and become something more. It has always been that way since the beginning of time.

The mystery of life, love, birth, death, beauty, joy even pain and suffering speak to us in another language. Words cannot fully express what we sense or feel. All we can do is to be there, be embraced by the moment and know that God has touched our lives again.

We say our God is one and yet our God is three. We say God is like a family. But there is more. There will always be more. We cannot truly understand the mystery of our God. If we did we would be God. Our understanding of God must not only be an exercise of the mind but also an awareness of the heart and a strengthening of our imaginations.

Jesus has told us that He is the revelation of the Father's love. To know Him is to know the Father. Like any Father worthy of the name, God provides and cares for His family. He feels what they feel. He shares in their joys and sorrows, their success and failures. He is always there, in the good times as well as the bad. Our God is a compassionate God. And Jesus is the sign of that compassion.

We say that God is transcendent, above and beyond and yet He is within all of creation, within you and within me. In some beautiful and mysterious way we share in His very life because we are created in His image and likeness. In other words we share in those magnificent powers of knowing and loving. To know is to love and to love is to become one with the beloved.

We say that it is the Spirit that empowers us to act in a God-like way. The Holy Spirit is the advocate, the Paraclete, the source of all our holiness. It is the same Spirit that prompts us to bring about the kingdom, to be a sign of God's love for all that the Father has created. Jesus showed us how to live and how to die, doing the Father's will. It is His Spirit that gives us the power to do what we are to do as His followers. But there is more; there will always be more.

The God we know is the God we experience each and every day of our lives. If we are too busy doing and have forgotten how to be, we will miss the God who wants to break into our hectic lives to surprise us and make us aware of His love. If we are too busy worrying about tomorrow we will miss the beauty of today, the flowers of the field and the birds of the air that neither work nor toil. If we never appreciate the gifts and well timed events of our day, we will never rejoice in the goodness of our God who delights in His children, each and everyone of us. In every experience of life we are to seek and find the God who creates us, saves us and sanctifies us, the God who makes us one in His love.

Jesus again reminds us as He did His disciples. I have much more to tell you but you cannot bear it now. Jesus knows our limitations, our humanness. He knows our search for truth and happiness. His Spirit will guide and direct us in His ways. That is His promise to all who are baptized in His name. What evidence will you show of His love this coming week? Happy Heavenly Father's day and happy fathers' day to all you Dads. God bless!

Corpus Christi B – Sacred Meal Sunday

Scripture: Exodus 24:3-8, Hebrews 9:11-15, Mark 14:12-16, 22-26

Whenever we celebrate something special in our lives we mark the event with a meal, inviting family and friends. We have birthday parties and funeral luncheons. We have wedding dinners and graduation gatherings. We have jubilees, anniversaries, ordinations and receptions of all kinds, retirement dinners and also farewells. All these times of celebrations are events of joy and happiness, sometimes sadness and sorrow but always a promise of something new, something more. It is this sharing in a meal that again strengthens and encourages us as we journey through life. We feed not only our bodies but also our spirits.

On the night before He died, Jesus gathered with His friends in that Upper Room where they celebrated a meal together. It was the Passover Supper, which marked their freedom from slavery. It was also in this context that Jesus took bread, blessed it and broke it. "Take this", He said, "This is My Body". He likewise took the cup. "This is my blood", the blood of the new covenant, which will be poured out for many, For more than two thousand years now, you and I have been gathering in His name to do this in memory of Him.

That is why we are here this morning. People all over our world share in this common meal, the Body and Blood of the Risen Lord. However, if we are people of faith what we eat and drink must have an effect in our lives. The Eucharist is to transform us into the likeness of the One we profess to love. What did the Lord say? The person who feeds on my flesh and drinks my blood abides in Me and I in him. And yes, there is more. We endorse what was said by the people of Israel: "All that God has said we will do."

There is nothing magical or automatic about our reception of the Eucharist. If we do not know what we are receiving and most importantly why we are receiving the Body and Blood of the Risen Lord, then very little will happen to change the way we live. To nourish ourselves on Jesus, the Bread of Life means more than just receiving bread and drinking from the cup. It means believing Him with all of our minds, loving Him with all our hearts, following Him with all of our wills. When we feed on Him in that way, He will be all that we need to build His kingdom of love here in our little corner of the world.

Jesus intended that the Eucharist be something that we are and not just something we do here in church. We are to be His members, His hands and feet, His eyes and His ears, His arms reaching out in love. Jesus not only told the good news to others He really was that good news and He wants us to be that same good news to all those we meet each and every day. We are gifts to one another and what we say and do has consequences on the lives of others.

At each Eucharist we celebrate we offer our thanksgiving for all that has been and we look to the future toward all that will be. Each Eucharist unites us one to another as brothers and sisters in the Lord. We are empowered to serve as the Lord has served, to heal as the Lord has healed, and to rejoice as He rejoiced. In Him we find the courage to carry our cross as He carried His, to love as He has loved, laying down His life for you and for me. Even though we are many, we become one in the sharing of the one bread and the one cup.

At each Eucharist we make our return to the Lord for all He has lovingly given to us. We take up the Cup of Salvation and eat of the Bread of Life. We call upon the name of the Lord in joy and thanksgiving. The Eucharist is our nourishment on the journey of life. We are what we eat. We are the Body of Christ! God bless.

12th OT B – Fear Sunday

Scripture: Job 38:1, 8-11, 2 Corinthians 5:14-17, Mark 4:35-41

All of us know that life is fragile and easily broken. We are made painfully aware of that each day when we watch the six o'clock news or hear about the latest suffering or tragic death of some one we know. We are frightened by the unknown and it is a good thing we are. We are warned that to lead a careless and reckless life is to flirt with death.

However, we are not to be overcome by our fears but to use them to protect and preserve our lives. Fear makes cowards of us all and cowards we know die a thousand deaths. Fear becomes a source of strength when we are people of faith, people who believe and trust in God's providence, His care and His love.

The gospel story we hear this beautiful morning is all about fear. The crossing of the Sea of Galilee was not an unusual trip. These fishermen had crossed it many times before but this would be a trip they would never forget. Somewhere in the middle of the sea and in the middle of the night, they were caught in a terrible fierce storm. They did not think they would ever make it. "Doesn't it matter to You Lord that we are going to drown?" "Why are you so frightened, so afraid? Be still," He said. The winds died down and all became calm. "Who is this?" they asked. "Even the wind and the sea obey Him?"

The purpose that Mark had in mind in writing this story was to encourage and strengthen the early Church which at that time was undergoing much suffering, persecution, doubt and despair, a Church not unlike our own these days. Even though the Lord seems to be silent, asleep, even though He seems not aware of their plight, He is still with them. All they have to do is to call upon His name and all will be well. They have the power to overcome all fear, all evil and every darkness.

Fear is a good and healthy reminder of our human frailty and limitations. Sooner or later in life all of us experience unexpected storms and it seems as though we will never make it through the night. Sometimes it is the very darkness of the night that will not afford a glimmer of light. There is no hope and we wonder if God is aware of our struggle, if He has abandoned us and left us to our fate. Although God may be silent and hidden, His presence is no less real. We know Him during those good times. Why is He not there also during those bad times or dark and difficult days? Evil is not a sign of His absence but the very force that He has come to destroy. This is a good thought to ponder.

Jesus was subject to all kinds of fear and evil. As scripture so often reminds us, He was exactly like us in all things but sin. He freely gave Himself over to evil men and accepted death on a cross crying out in one of His last statements wondering why the Father had forsaken Him. Yet, He let go of all that fear and accepted in faith the Father's will.

Real faith is also a trust in God's care in the very midst of difficulty or disaster. We are never beyond God's reach despite the raging waters and winds that threaten our very lives. Even though we may be tossed about by worry and fear we have a Master and Lord who can quiet our stormy minds and restless hearts.

The secret of this faith and trust is learned each and every day and not only during those stormy times of our lives. We are to know, trust and appreciate the goodness of our God, His providence and care for all that He has created. You and I travel in good company, Jesus the Lord of life Himself. God bless.

13th OT B – Death Sunday

Scripture: Wisdom 1:13-15, 2:23-24, 2 Corinthians 8:7, 9, 13-15, Mark 5:21-43

It seems that death comes when we least expect it. It does not matter how old or how young a person is or how sick he or she might be. The scriptures tell us that death comes like a thief in the night and it steals away someone we love. Death frightens all of us and makes us sad. We want to live, to go on forever. God has planted that hope, that dream deep in our hearts.

This morning we heard from the book of wisdom that God did not make death nor does He rejoice in the destruction of the living. He fashioned all things that they might have being. He formed us to be imperishable. He made us in His own image and likeness. The nature of our God is that He lives forever. The Father of us all has sent His Son to tell us that life is so good, so beautiful, and so precious that not even death can overcome it.

This is what the miracle story is all about. The official, Jarius had no one to turn to; "Please come," he begs the Lord of life. Come and lay your hands upon her so that she might get well and live. Jesus is moved by his faith but by the time they arrive, we are told that the little girl has died. What a tragedy, we would say. There is nothing quite as sad as the death of a young child. In their sadness and despair they said:" Don't trouble the teacher any longer. There is nothing more to be done". But there is: Jesus said; "Do not be afraid, just have faith." And we know what happened. He took the little girl by the hand and she got up. They could not believe their eyes. Death is not to have its final say. Jesus, the Lord of life reminds us once again that love is stronger than death itself.

This miracle story speaks to us about that love. God does not love according to the world's rules or regulations. He is not restricted in what He can or cannot do for each of us. He is not limited in His power, nor His wisdom, nor care, concern or love. And that is why we are called to be people of faith, people who trust in that love knowing that our God is with us and not against us. It is our faith that opens up our minds and hearts to know that love. It is our faith that will help us to let go and let God be God for us. He truly wants to be our Father. We need to be reminded that this letting go is a day by day experience. It is a dying to selfishness, sin and my way of doing things in order to follow the Lord in His ways.

As people of faith, followers of the Lord of Life, we are called to reach out and touch the lives of others. There is something life -giving in our helping others in their need whatever it might be. Who among us has not known pain and suffering? What person has never been touched by sickness, separation and sorrow? Who among us does not know doubt, discouragement, despair and even death itself? It is our faith that tells us that we must be like the Lord of Life, truly compassionate and caring for one another. Paul reminds us once again: Jesus made Himself poor that we might become rich in the knowledge of God's love and so find the fullness of life. When you and I reach out to others in their poorness, we enrich their lives and assure them of our Father's love.

We begin another new month and it is the fourth of July and we will be with family and friends in celebration. We are also reminded of the sacrifice that many have made for the price of freedom. What an opportunity to fill our gatherings with joy, renewed hope, trust and faith in our God. It really is our life-giving words and actions that heal and bring out the best in others. God bless.

14th OT B – Disappointment Sunday

Scripture: Ezekiel 2:2-5, 2 Corinthians 12:7-10, Mark 6:1-6

Isn't it strange how life has a way of shattering many of our hopes and dreams? We plan a special weekend for family and friends and would you believe it. It rains for forty days! We have great expectations for a son or daughter and they decide to do things their own way. We have a great opportunity for a bigger and better job and someone else is hired. Life is filled with all kinds of disappointments from simple broken dreams to broken hearts. It is all part of the fabric of every day living in the real world.

It is very interesting to see how Jesus dealt with the disappointments of life. He had begun His public ministry and the response had been enthusiastic, at times even overwhelming. He was excited about what was happening and decided to return home to his native Nazareth to bring them the good news. His life-long neighbors and relatives listened to His teachings and were impressed. But instead of responding to the message they began to wonder about the messenger. "Isn't He the carpenter, the son of Mary? Don't we know His brothers and sisters? Now, where did He get all this?" He was just too much for them. The scripture goes on to tell us: And because of their lack of faith, He was not able to do much good in His hometown.

The one thing He wanted more than anything else was a generous response to this good news. It seemed as though they were curious about this native Son, even amazed by Him. But they were not ready to accept those new and crazy ideas. He had asked too much of them and they were unwilling to change. Of course Jesus was disappointed and who wouldn't be? No prophet is without honor, except in his native place, among his own kindred and in his own house. He needed a reminder that life had not singled him out as a failure. Many of the earlier prophets had also been rejected and ignored. Many modern day prophets suffer the same fate. They had a cause and because they spoke an unpopular truth, they suffered and paid dearly. Jesus was able to understand what was happening and He did not see all this as a total rejection. It really said that He was numbered among those great and influential people, the prophets of old. Maybe Jesus was disappointed but He was not discouraged. In fact, He was more determined to make the best out of a disappointing situation and that I think is the challenge He presents to you and me this day.

Mark goes on to say: He could work no miracle there apart from curing a few who were sick. He was unable to help the many but He was able to help the few. Rather than be disappointed about all that could be done, He would do as much as He was able. Even though His preaching in Nazareth was mostly a failure, it was not a total loss.

I think the same wisdom applies to your life and my life. Whenever we have to settle for something less than our hopes and dreams, we can go on to make the most of what has been given.

Like all people, Jesus who shares our human nature, knows all of our pain and suffering of disappointment. But unlike many, He was not defeated by it. He accepted that reality and did what He could, and then moved on to the next thing that life had to offer. We all know that disappointments are part of life and we can expect them. By following the Lord's example, we can make the best out of those experiences for the Lord is always with us in the bad times as well as the good. It is our faith that assures us of His presence.

I remember a wise old man at Medicare in Manistique. He would always tell me: "Keep on keeping on and the Good Lord will take a liking to you!" There is much wisdom in that statement. God bless.

15th OT B – Chosen Sunday

Scripture: Amos 7:12-15, Ephesians 1:3-14, Mark 6:7-13

There is something very special about being chosen. We feel honored, respected and unique because we are able to offer our gifts and talents for a worthy cause. We become part of a team that works toward a common goal. We help to accomplish that task and purpose and we feel fulfilled and find our happiness. There are several good examples of that right here in our hometown; I think of the Lions and all the good they have done over their years; the VFW who keep alive a patriotic spirit; the many people who worked hard to turn the old Ejay theater into what it is today. And who can forget the many fine women of our parish who continue to serve funeral breakfasts and do so many fine things building up the parish; the Knights of Columbus; the St. Vincent de Paul. And the list of good things accomplished could go on and on.

All of the scriptures on this beautiful evening remind us how we have been chosen, that we are special, unique and have dignity as sons and daughters of a loving Father. God has called us and chosen us from the very first moment of life in our mother's womb. Paul goes on to say that all of us have been chosen not only the prophets and priests. All of us have been chosen through Christ to be brothers and sisters with Him and one another. In fact, we have been sealed with the Holy Spirit so that we might see the hope to which we are called. We are to be holy and blameless in His sight; full of love.

In the call of Amos, the shepherd and farmer, we are reminded that God has called us just as we are. We don't have to belong to a special group or have a degree or even be gifted by some rare skill or talent. We need not be perfect or sinless. We have been chosen and called as we are to do the work of the Lord. Like the twelve, who were ordinary and simple people, we have been summoned to proclaim that the reign of God is in our midst and from our own experience we know that is no easy task.

The scripture goes on to tell us that Jesus summoned the twelve and gave them authority but it was not the power of force or fear. No, their authority would come from their willingness to model their lives after Jesus, to be true to His personal example. In other words their strength or power would come from being authentic, that is true, real and honest. There is to be no pretending, no saying one thing and doing another, and no bad or poor example. Someone once said:

Who we are and what we do speaks so loudly that others cannot hear what we are saying. The media is really the message! It is our authenticity that is at the heart of teaching and healing, the work of the kingdom. We are authentic when we are consistent, when what we are is what we do and that means that being a disciple of the Lord is not just limited to one action but rather is a whole way of being. It is a way of life. The early Christians were said to belong to "the way". We are authentic when we are compassionate, when we suffer along with others and that means that we not only feel their pain and suffering but that we do something about their anguish. We match our words with our deeds.

The gospel story also reminds us that we are to be free from the non-essentials and simply get down to the business of building God's kingdom instead of feathering our own nest. We are authentic when we live unencumbered lives, not caught up with things, with power, prestige and money or a life style contrary to gospel values.

Like those sent by the Lord, we are to wear the sandals of simplicity and take along the walking stick of trust and confidence to support us on the way. Our call to be holy and blameless in the sight of God is surprisingly simple. We are to be authentic Christians; the beautiful people God has called and chosen us to be. The reign of God will happen through us as we do ordinary things in an extraordinary way.

In your family gatherings or in the market place of every day living what will you do to bring about the kingdom of our loving God during this coming week? God Bless

16th OT B – Shepherd Sunday

Scripture: Jeremiah 23:1-6, Ephesians 2: 13-18, Mark 6:30-34

Whenever I think about sheep without a shepherd, I think of all those lost souls that wander aimlessly through life not knowing about God's care, concern and His love. I think of all those caught up with drugs and alcohol, greed and selfishness. Or those so busy acquiring things and getting ahead that they never find time for family or friends, let alone their God. I think of the poor, the homeless, all those unemployed or without a sufficient income. Sometimes I think we are the poorest of the poor because we need nothing and still want everything!

We often forget that Jesus is our Good Shepherd who guides us in right paths and will be with us in the darkest hours, day in and day out, till the end of our lives. It seems to me that we all need an out of the way place for a little rest, a little time to be with the Lord.

When Jesus saw the crowds of people, pushing and shoving, hoping to see and hear Him or perhaps to be healed or fed, Mark said: "He pitied them." They were like sheep without a shepherd, not knowing where to turn. The scripture goes on to tell us He began to teach them, to lead them out so that they might experience God's care and love, His salvation. He taught them with parables, allowing them to discover the truth about life. He freed them from a quick and easy solution to all their problems and needs. He showed them how to find their God. He was able to do this because He had done it for Himself. He would offer that same personal wholeness to all those searching for the fullness of life. Because Jesus was in touch with His Father, knowing the power of God in Him, He was able to call forth that same power dwelling in others. That really is the secret of life, isn't it? God dwelling within us and we finding the faith, hope and trust to let go and let God be God for us. Only when we have found the Lord can we become busy about His kingdom.

Before we can begin that good work, we must realize that we will never satisfy our hearts as long as we continue to look outside of ourselves. Happiness, wholeness and holiness come from within and not from things, not from money, not even from power or prestige. Our salvation comes only when we are led to the very center of our being, when the God within can speak to our hearts. It is when we find our true self that we discover that power. When we take time, make a little space in our busy lives for the Lord, we will then find the necessary strength, courage and determination to continue the work of the kingdom.

When Jesus and His friends reached the other side they were surprised to see the same faces they had just left. There they were, waiting for them. It was unfortunate that they had so little time to spend together but it was just enough time to be renewed and refreshed so that they were able to take up the work of the kingdom once again. These people were like sheep without a shepherd.

Being human we are all vulnerable, we are easily confused and hurt. As much as we live out of our false self we have a tendency to show ourselves as self-assured and quite stable mentally. The tiniest of microbes can bring about poor health; the betrayal of a friend can do serious damage to our hearts; the loss of a reputation betrays our very being.

We need not look too far to find these same familiar, wandering people. They are in your family, or just down the street, maybe even next door or at your place of work. They too are waiting. They wait for your care, your patience, your compassion and love. They may be waiting for someone to encourage them and give them a second chance. Just as the Good Shepherd has shepherded us so we are called to shepherd one another. Have you seen any good

shepherds lately? God bless

There is a lad here who has five barley loaves and
a couple of dried fish.

17th OT B – Share Sunday

Scripture: 2 Kings 4:42-44, Ephesians 4:1-6, John 6:1-15

There are many thousands of people who go to bed hungry every night. These are mostly starving children in every nation of our world. It is sad to see their tiny little bodies wasting away, their stomachs distended because of lack of nourishment. Sickness and death usually follows. I read something very interesting the other day: Out of ten children in our world, three of them load their plates with whatever they like, including most of the meat and fish, milk and eggs and then they throw into the garbage can what they cannot eat. Two other children somehow manage to meet their basic needs. Three more children avoid the pain of starvation with a handful of rice or beans and some bread. The last two children die before the evening of each and every day of the year. Isn't that terrible?

In spite of all of our technological advances and great progress in agriculture we still have not been able to find ways to share what we have with those in need. What can we do? You may ask. Jesus asked the same question. "Where can we buy enough food for them to eat? "Not even with two hundred days wages could we buy loaves enough to give each one of them a morsel," Philip responded. Andrew then suggested: "There is a lad here who has five barley loaves and a couple of fish but what good is that for so many?" Then Jesus took the bread and fish and in some mysterious and beautiful way He fed over five thousand people. There was more than enough to satisfy their every need. In fact, they gathered twelve baskets of food that was left over. They could not believe their eyes. The scripture goes on to tell us that they wanted to make Him King. But he wanted no part of that. He fled back to the mountain to be alone.

You are probably wondering: How did Jesus ever feed so many people with just a few loaves of bread and some fish? Most of our modern day scripture scholars see this miracle not so much as an unlimited supply of food from that meager offering but as a miracle of sharing. When Jesus blessed and broke that bread something happened; something beautiful happened! It was not to the loaves and fish but to the hearts of those present. Following the example of that little boy, one by one they began to share with one another the little they secretly and selfishly had for themselves. There was more than enough for all. They were totally satisfied. The greatest miracle to me is the fact that all present were willing to share what they had with those who did not have enough. Now isn't that what the kingdom of God is all about? Isn't it about sharing our lives, who we are and what we have with all the hungry of our own little world. The Lord would remind us that salvation is here in this place and not only in the hereafter.

There are many hungry in Africa, India, and in South America. Yes, even here in our own land of plenty people are ill fed and clothed. There are many starving for our care, our concern and our love right where we are, perhaps in our own families, next door or just down the street. They hunger for your friendship, your understanding, your encouragement and affirmation. Who are they? They are our young and our old, all sorts of people who are dying for someone to share their faith, their hope and love so that they might know that life is worth living.

When you think about it, all of us are hungry. That is why we are here. The Eucharist we share nourishes our faith, hope and love. It is the Lord of Life who will more than satisfy the hungers of the human heart. What more do we desire; knowing God's love and His daily bread? Our hearts' desire is to share what we have received with all those who come to us in their need. God bless.

He was transfigured before their eyes.

Transfiguration Sunday B

Scripture: Daniel 7:9-10, 13-14, 2 Peter 1:16-19, Mark 9:2-10

We take a short break from ordinary time to celebrate the Feast of the Transfiguration, which is also celebrated during the season of Lent. Jesus is transfigured in all of His glory before His three close friends; Peter, James and John. It was a peak experience for them. They suddenly realized and finally accept that Jesus will suffer, die and rise again on the third day. They were not only dazzled by all the light but they themselves were changed. I think it is most important to keep in mind that this is a post resurrection story written long after Jesus' rising from the dead.

It is interesting: Peter for the first time in his life is speechless. "This is My Beloved Son. Listen to Him." Now they knew; through suffering and death, through failure there is a new life, the promise of salvation. Usually we think of Jesus' transfiguration as a triumph of glory and that is what it is but there is more, much more. Jesus accepted His ultimate failure, His death on a cross. For Him the two went hand in hand, first death then glory. How often we hear from sacred scripture that Jesus learned obedience from the things He suffered.

The first reading from Daniel also speaks of transfiguration and change. The people of that time period had been subject to all kinds of suffering from their cruel and intolerant neighbors. Daniel was to assure them that the day would come when God would overcome their darkness and despair with an everlasting reign that will conquer all evil. He encouraged them to believe, to open their eyes to see what would happen. Hidden in the midst of every darkness, there are beacons of hope!

In that second reading from Peter we recognize some of the words from the Gospel. The point really is made. Who was changed? It certainly was not Jesus. He was simply revealed as the one He had always been. His three friends were changed and transformed.

We are to be changed by learning obedience to the hard facts of life from the things that we also suffer. It is a blessing if we learn to accept failure as a necessary part of life instead of being surprised by it or trying to find some easy solution for all of our suffering. But we never come to terms with these lesser failures until we recognize and accept the ultimate failure of death.

All of us know that sooner or later we are going to die. But we pretend that it won't happen for a long time. Maybe it will when I am eight-three or so. We separate death from life itself when it is part of the fabric of life hereafter. Yet every day we die a little and each year brings us closer to the grave. We are scared of death and try to make something eternal. Love is forever we say and it is. But sometimes it isn't. Maybe it was not love after all. Maybe love just died.

We like to think that our children will comfort us in our old age, that they will carry on our name and all that we worked so hard for. And they should but sometimes they don't. Maybe it is not their fault. Maybe it is because all of us are orphans and strangers born out of due time.

Children like to think their parents are perfect. And they ought to be. But sometimes they are not. It is not because they don't want to be but just because no one is. Parents can fail their children. But when we bury our parents we also recognize their humanness along with their love and we love them all the more.

All of us know that life is good, beautiful and precious. We all want to be millionaires. However, we need to also realize that life's failures are just as important as all of our successes. We are all losers as well as winners at times. But there is something sacred and timeless, something that never fails. It is our God. God takes all of our failures in hand and makes them whole. To experience and know His presence in our failures gives us the courage to go on.

You and I are to learn obedience from the things we suffer along the way. We live and learn how to die to our selfishness and sin and finally let go and leave the mystery of life to our loving God.

In a moment you and I will share in the Eucharist, the one bread and cup that makes us one in Christ. That bread and wine has been transformed into the body and blood of the Risen Christ. This Eucharist as does every one we celebrate calls each of us to be transformed and transfigured into the One we profess to love. God Bless.

19th OT B – Trust Sunday

Scripture: 1 Kings 19:4-8, Ephesians 4:30 - 5:2, John 6:41-51

We all have our days when nothing seems to go right. Some people have weeks that go that way. Sometimes it looks like a whole life-time is spent with pain, suffering and tragedy of all sorts. There is a mystery about life, about suffering and death that we will never fully understand. Sometimes we murmur. Sometimes we complain. Sometimes we are just plain tired and worn out. We need a rest and a change.

Like Elijah in that first reading we would like to run away and hide. It was no easy task to be a prophet. The people did not listen. He was misunderstood and not appreciated. We know that they drove him out of town. After a day's journey into the desert, he was too tired to even live. He prayed for death. "That's enough Lord. I can't take it anymore." But Elijah's God would not let him give up and die. God gave him food and a good night's rest and Elijah was able to travel forty days and nights to the mountain of God. It is there on that mountain that he will meet God and we read later on that God strengthens and encourages him to return to the people who had just rejected him.

With all of our problems, our heartaches and headaches it is easy to not appreciate that Elijah's God is also our God. Our God is with us on those days when the sun does not shine as well as those days of happiness when things are going well. Our God is a God of life, not death, a God of forgiveness and not revenge, a God of love not hatred, a God of peace, justice, mercy and compassion. Our God has begun a good work in us and He will see that good work brought to its completion. That will happen if we are people of faith, people who know Jesus as the Bread of Life, people who strive to live out those ideals and values that He has given us.

In John's gospel which was written many years after the Resurrection, people come to faith not so much because of what Jesus said and did but because of who He is. Jesus is the revelation of the Father's compassion, mercy and love for each of us. He is the Son of God who freely lays down His life for you and for me. Jesus is our Brother who shows us the Way, evidences the Truth in the way He lived and the Life that knows no limits or bounds. Jesus is the Bread of life and those that eat of this Bread identify with His way of life. It is this Bread of life that will sustain us as we journey to the mountain of our

God. You and I are called to be people of faith, whose hope and trust are in the Lord and His ways, who know His love and want to respond by loving others as He has loved us.

As a pilgrim people on our way, Paul has some important advice as we travel: "Do nothing to sadden the Holy Spirit." We are to rid ourselves of all bitterness, anger, harsh words and malice of every kind. In place of all these means things we are to bring life to others by our kindness, forgiveness, mercy and compassion. We are challenged to follow the way of love every day.

Jesus is the pattern and the example of what we are called to be. By eating of the Bread of Life we are nourished and strengthened for all of the trials and tribulations that life can offer. In our communion with Him we bring His good news into the market place of everyday living. God bless.

20th OT – B Bread of life Sunday

Scripture: Proverbs 9:1-6, Ephesians 5:15-20, John 6:51-58

We are a hungry people, a people starving for life; not a drab, dreary , dull existence but a people who long for the fullness of life, the very best that life can offer, here and now, each day and of course life hereafter. There is a famine in this rich, great and prosperous land and many people do not know which way to go. To whom shall they turn? How will they ever satisfy their hunger? "Our hearts are restless", one of our great saints remarked, "They are restless until our hearts rest in you, my God!"

This evening we hear Jesus tell the crowds: "I Myself am the living bread come down from heaven. The bread I will give is My flesh for the life of the world". But they did not understand what He meant. They had just eaten the bread and fish He had broken for them. They thought this would satisfy their hunger but it did not. They came back for more. Now Jesus would offer them a share in His very being. .Jesus often spoke of Himself as word, as bread, as water and as wine. But a word once spoken is lost if no one hears it said. Bread offered and not eaten becomes dry or it gets moldy. Water and wine are poured out and must be drunk or it will become warm and stale. Jesus offers Himself to all people. However, if they chose not to accept His offer, they will not find happiness or the fullness of life. In other words, sharing in Jesus' body and blood we are led to eternal life, but it only comes through the cross. By eating and drinking of the Body and Blood of the Lord, we freely choose to become that which we consume. We also are to be broken open, poured out, shared for the life of the world.

For some of His followers, this was a hard saying and the scripture goes on to tell us that many could not follow in His ways. There are many who still do not understand what He meant. There are some who look upon the Eucharist as an object to be received rather than a way of life to be lived. Whenever we eat His flesh and drink His blood we are caught up into Christ, a total intimacy, a complete sharing of life with life. That is hard to understand but let's look at it further. His thoughts are to become our thoughts. His feelings are to be our feelings. His attitude of doing things according to the Father's will is to be our attitude. Doing the Father's will is not to be a sad cry of "its God's will" but rather God's will is to bring us to the joy of our heart's desire. Remember God knows us, the best in us as well as the worst and God accepts us just as we are.

Maybe you are thinking that all of this is very hard to understand. Yes, it is really a mystery. We are called to be people of faith, people who are willing to risk and trust that kind of intimacy with the Lord. At each Eucharist we share all of our hopes and dreams, all of our doubts and worries, all of our pain and suffering and join ourselves to Him who is the victor over all suffering and sin, all pain and even death itself.

In faith we celebrate life eternal now, not only after we die. All we need do is to recognize our hunger, know our emptiness and then open our hearts to receive His gift and be filled with His love.

Our life in the Risen Lord is not something we watch from a distance. It is something we enter into. The waters of baptism are poured on our heads and we get wet. We break open our lives to our own sinfulness and we embrace God's mercy, forgiveness and reconciliation. We feed on the Body and Blood of the Lord and we are energized to new life. We gather in His name this day to give thanks and remember. God Bless.

21st OT B – Only Choice Sunday

Scripture: Joshua 24:1-2a, 15-17, 18b, Ephesians 5:21-32, John 6:60-69

There is a beautiful point and bay on the north shore of Lake Michigan called *Seul Choix*. Maybe you know it well. It was the early French explorers that named it. For *Seul Choix* means the only choice. In their travels by boat from St. Ignace to Manistique it was the only choice they could make if a sudden storm came up. The lake could become very violent and stormy and their only safety was to seek refuge beyond that point into the sheltered harbor. There they could wait out the storm and later continue on their way.

In the Gospel reading this morning we hear how Simon Peter makes his only choice. "Lord to whom shall we go? You alone have the words of eternal life. We have come to believe." And even more: "We are convinced that you are the Holy One of God." Peter knows in faith that Jesus has the words of everlasting life, that He will be a safe refuge and shelter from all the storms of life. By following in the Lord's way he will find the joy, the peace, the happiness and the love his heart longs for.

Everyday you and I are faced with many choices or decisions. Some are easy to make because there is little risk involved. Others are decisions that will alter or change the course of our lives; to go on to college or to join the service, to marry now or wait till later, to buy this house or to rent, to move to a larger town or to stay here, to retire or keep on working. Sooner or later we must choose whom or what we will serve.

In our first reading today we heard Joshua tell the people: "Decide whom you will serve. As for me and my household we will serve the Lord." After remembering all the Lord had done for them, the people responded: "We also will serve the Lord for He is our God!"

During these busy days there are many people who choose to serve their own gods. Some are self-serving, choosing only wealth, power, fame or honor. They are the ones who say: "You only go around once so get all you can out of life." They love things and use people when it should be the other way around. They can hardly wait to win the lottery or spend hours at the casino. They love the weekends when they have time to do their thing. Their gods are never satisfied and so they find life dull, boring and many times unhappy. They only look for one good time after another and never stop to ask themselves; what is life all about?

But there are others who are devoted to their families, who are loyal to their friends, who are dedicated to serving others just as they serve their God. You know them. They are people of faith not fear; people of hope and not despair. They are people of love not selfishness and greed. They are the people of service who give of their time, their talent and treasure and do not count the cost. Yes, you know them. They bring joy, peace, happiness and love into our lives. They have made the only choice. They serve the Lord for He is their God. In faith they know that Jesus is that only choice for He has the words of everlasting life.

It is not easy to follow this Jesus! It is risky business and His words are sometimes hard to endure. There is always some doubt, some uneasiness about what will happen next. We are never sure of the outcome or the price that we may have to pay. To accept who and what Jesus is all about demands a great deal of faith, trust, faithfulness and a promise of a new tomorrow. The moment of decision is not a once in a life time experience but rather a day by day choice to follow in His ways. God bless.

22nd OT B – Pharisee Sunday

Scripture: Deuteronomy 4:1-2, 6-8, James 1:17-18, 21b-22, 27 Mark 7:1-8, 14-15, 21-23

It is so easy to get locked into one way of looking at life. There almost seems to be pattern to follow and everyone is expected to go through the same routine. We have our rules and regulations, all kinds of rituals to be observed. There is the right way and the wrong way and we are expected to do it right. Now if you follow all these rules and regulations you will be successful. All this is sometimes referred to as conventional wisdom. But Jesus has a better idea about life. He tells us that we are unique, individual, and special with gifts and talents that make us one of a kind. God has made us that way. Jesus would have us become that beautiful person God has called us to be.

The Scribes and Pharisees, those experts in the law failed to understand that important truth. We hear them ask: "How come your disciples do not wash their hands? Why don't they follow the rules and regulations set down by the church?" How can they be members of that church when they ignore those all important laws, those rules and regulations? The Lord had a lot to say about that kind of religious thinking. True religion is not defined by following rules and regulations or giving lip service, saying one thing and doing another. To be clean or unclean is not a matter of hands but rather a matter of the heart.

Mark has Jesus quoting Isaiah: "Empty is the reverence due to God because rules and regulations have become their god. No, it is not that out there, those external things that make one unfit for the kingdom. It is all those wicked designs, that obtuse spirit that comes from within and so affects the way you live."

I often wonder what an obtuse spirit really is. It sounds terrible and not only that, an obtuse spirit is in opposition to all that Jesus would expect us to have or to be. I think it comes from some of that same pharisaical thinking. It is really an arrogant spirit, "a know it all" personality. You know what I mean. It goes like this: If I fulfill all those rules and regulations, all those Sunday rituals, then I have satisfied my obligation to God and God now has to do His part. If I keep the law and you do not; then that is great for me, but too bad for you. You just don't measure up to God's expectations. After all if I follow the rules and regulations God can't expect any more from me. I have done my part.

Don't you find it interesting how a religion of laws has all the answers to the mystery of life and can easily explain away any problem, difficulty and suffering? We know deep in our hearts that life is just not that way. Our God is a God of love and His love shines on the unjust as well as the just. We know that God has no favorites. His love is freely given to all and it is to be freely received by all. How senseless it is to think that we can earn His love by obeying rules and regulations. We are not in business with God. To receive His love is to live in His love. The only response that we can make is to love in return.

James tells us in that second reading: "We are to humbly welcome the word that has taken root in us." We just don't listen to that word. We ponder and reflect upon it and then act on that word at every opportunity we have. The God who has created us in His image sees into our hearts and finds the good that is there. The Lord who redeemed us with His blood looks into our hearts and finds His own life reflected there. The Spirit who dwells within our hearts gathers us around this table this day to nourish us and send us forth to live out the Good News we have received. God bless.

23rd OT B – Deaf and Dumb Sunday

Scripture: Isaiah 35:4-7a, James 2:1-5, Mark 7:31-37

Someone once said that every age, culture or society has three kinds of people: those who make things happen, those who watch things happen and those who wonder what happened? When it comes to our response as followers of the Lord, very few make things happen, most watch what happens and still many others wonder what happened. In a recent survey in the Church, thirty eight percent of parents felt very sure when they spoke to their children about God, religious beliefs and values. That means that sixty two percent are unable to tell their own flesh and blood what they believe in and live for. It seems as though we do not make things happen. We now merely watch them happen. Very soon lacking a miracle, we will be wondering what happened in our world. We ask and wonder who is deaf and dumb!

This evening we hear about Jesus, the Miracle Worker who opens the ears of the deaf man and loosens his tongue to speak. The people are amazed. For Mark, Jesus is the One who has come to liberate those who are frightened, those who are blind and cannot see, those who are deaf and we would say all those who hear but do not listen. Jesus is the one for all those who cannot speak because they are afraid to voice their thinking. The first and most important aspect of being free is to realize that we are in bondage. All of us are in need of healing and salvation. It is the sick who have need of the doctor. It is the sinner that has need of forgiveness. It is the ignorant who have need for education. It is the lover that has a need to express care, concern and love for others. We must first recognize our needs before we can do something about them. It is interesting to note that it is the friends of the deaf man who bring him to Jesus for healing. Without their help, he is helpless. Jesus is now able to lay His hands on him. "*Ephphatha*", that is: " be opened!" At once the man was free and he began to speak plainly.

There are times when we don't hear the cries of those around us. It isn't that we cannot hear. It is because we do not really listen with compassion to what they are saying. Why is it that we tune people out and fail to hear what they are saying? The worst possible answer could be that we do not care. But it is more likely that we do not listen because we are so preoccupied. We have our own problems, our own worries and troubles, our own conflicts to resolve.

To realize and recognize that is to know that others also suffer that same kind of hearing problem. If we listen to them we might even find a solution to our own heartaches and headaches. Listening is one of the most important things we do. The deaf man could not speak unless he first heard. He had to listen well to what was said before he could respond.

Most of us need to ask the Lord to do for us what He did for that deaf man. We could turn up our hearing aids instead of being selective and hearing only what we want to hear. Isn't this interesting? The deaf man could not listen because he was not able to hear. We cannot hear because we choose not to listen. If the Lord opened closed ears He can also open closed minds and hearts helping us learn how to listen especially to the cries of the poor. Teen age psychologists suggest that there would be fewer problems in our homes if we took time to listen to our children. Maybe that is why we are blessed with two ears and only one mouth! We are to listen twice as often as we speak. Maybe then we would become doers of the word instead of wondering what happened. God Bless.

24th OT B – Who am I? Sunday

Scripture: Isaiah 50:5-9a, James 2:14-18, Mark 8:27-35

All of us in one way or another spend a good deal of our lives searching for answers. We want to know all about life. What is its purpose? Where am I going? Who am I? What is life all about? What does God expect of me? Why is there suffering and pain? Why death if there is life? Why life if there is death? The more we search to find some of the answers, the more we continue to wonder, to ask and search. Life really is a mystery to be lived each and every day. Life is not a problem to be solved.

On this fall-like evening, the scriptures bring us to another turning point, a moment of truth in our lives. Who do they say this Jesus is? What is He all about? The leaders of His day, the crowds, even His close family, relatives and friends failed to understand Him. Some thought He was John the Baptizer, or maybe Elijah or one of the prophets. Jesus was not satisfied with those answers so He asked them again. "And you, who do you, say that I am?" After a long silence Peter has the courage to say: "You are the Messiah". Peter has the right answer but the wrong meaning, yes; I am the Messiah but not the kind you might expect. No, I am not going to fit into your expectations or your thinking about life. Mark then goes on to tell us: "The Son of Man had to suffer much, be rejected by the elders, chief priests and scribes, be put to death and rise in three days." But Peter covered his ears. He would hear none of that. No, Lord, that is not going to happen to you. You will not win any followers to your cause that way. No, there must be an easier way. No, be the One we think you are. But Jesus' response is strong, determined and right to the point. He is reminded again of those same temptations He experienced in the desert before He began His public ministry. No, Peter, you are not judging by God's standards but by man's. In other words Jesus was saying that it was His Father's will that was all important for Him. Jesus saw beyond the expectations of Peter and all those who wanted Him to establish Israel as a great nation. Instead Jesus would become the obedient servant of the Father and begin the work of the kingdom. He would freely and lovingly accept the cross so that we might find life. For no greater love has anyone than to lay down his life for another.

In life there are no short cuts. There is no easy way to go if we are to choose to follow the Lord. We must deny ourselves and take up our cross each day for the sake of the kingdom. We are to lose our lives if we are to save them. It is the very opposite of what we want to do. It is the opposite of what the world would tell us we must do. We are to go beyond the ordinary way of doing things to follow Jesus in an extraordinary manner. You and I are called to reflect in our lives the very image of the One we profess to love. We are to see the Lord's reflection in each other.

Whether we intend it or not, we tell the world who Jesus is by the way we live out our days. Our words and actions should not mislead others as to what we believe.

In the reading from St. James we heard him say: "What good is it, my brothers and sisters if someone says he has faith but does not have works!" Faith in itself if it does not have works is dead! It must be more than "have a good day!" Our faith challenges us to feed the hungry, clothe the naked and find shelter for those who live on the streets of our cities. If we are to find life we are to share life with others! God Bless.

25th OT B – Important Sunday

Scripture: Wisdom 2:12, 17-20, James 3:16—4:3, Mark 9:30-37

All of us have a great need and desire to be first, the center of all that happens. It is first place in football. It is the best grades in school. It is the best job at work. It is first in line before all the others. It is first out of the parking lot after Church is over. There is an old saying and it goes as follows: We want the front seat on the bus, the middle of the road and the back seat in Church. Isn't it rather strange that we would rather be served than spending our days serving and helping others in their need?

Once again on this Fall evening the scriptures try to open up our minds and hearts to a deeper understanding of what Jesus is all about. According to Mark, Jesus is not a wonder worker who has come to take away all pain and suffering or to make life easy. No, He is the Suffering Servant who freely gives His life as a ransom for many, a Man who has come to serve and not to be served. His disciples did not understand what He meant or maybe it was that they did not want to understand. They were afraid that it would eventually cost them something. Instead they chose to talk about other things. Who was the most important? They must have been embarrassed when Jesus asked them what they were discussing. After a period of silence, Jesus said to them: "If anyone wants to rank first, he must remain the last one of all. He must be the servant of all." I think it is important to notice that Jesus did not scold them or make them feel guilty. He knows what it is to be human. He knows the need we have to feel good about self, that we are special, good and unique in God's eyes. In order to make His point He stood a little child in their midst. A child is helpless, totally dependent, always in need of care, concern and love. A helpless child can return no favors nor even make demands upon others. A child can be ignored, neglected and even abused. For some even today children are to be seen and not heard. Sometimes children are just in the way.

Jesus goes on to say: "Whoever welcomes a child like this for My sake, welcomes Me and whoever welcomes Me, welcomes the One who sent Me." Now they understand what He meant and there is no further mention about who was the greatest among them. That little child represents all children, all people who are weak and helpless, all those who are dependent upon the care of others, all those we might see as not important or insignificant in our eyes. In God's eyes, we are all His children. Everyone is important; every life has meaning and purpose. It makes no difference, young or old, rich or poor, white or black, saint or sinner. We are all brothers and sisters in the Lord. We are all in need so there is no reason to be in competition trying to win God's favor. We are not in business with God nor can we get ahead of our neighbor.

James again this week has some words of wisdom. "Whenever you find jealousy and greed, an attitude of me first, you will find disharmony and every kind of wicked thing being done." He goes on to say that our own inner cravings are the cause of all of our problems, all of our unhappiness. The more we have, the more we want and think we need. Self-centered greed and selfishness will never ever be satisfied. Wisdom that comes from above makes for peace, is kindly and considerate, is full of compassion and shows itself by doing good. Each of us is to realize that we are responsible for something much larger than ourselves.

Yes, we are important in God's eyes. The big surprise is that the gifts and talents, the treasure we are make us important in the eyes of others. As followers of the Lord of Life, we are to receive, welcome and minister to others in His name. God bless.

26th OT B – Scandal Sunday

Scripture: Numbers 11:25-29, James 5:1-6, Mark 9:38-43, 45, 47-48

Every so often we hear people talking about "we" and "they", and I wonder who they really are. They do this but we would never do that. They never go to Church nor do they take time to share their time, talent or treasure for others. They are not interested in the kingdom but we are. They are so set in their ways that they will never change. Funny as it may sound but they are most often we! We like to make all kinds of distinctions, divisions and separations. Yet we are all one; all God's people, all included in His loving embrace, rich or poor, Moslem or Jew, Liberal or Conservative, Republican or Democrat, saint or sinner and the list of divisions can go on and on. Either you believe it or not but there is room in God's house for all of us.

The Scriptures on this October weekend have much to tell us about being included, that we are all members of God's family that we are to reach out in loving service embracing all as brothers and sisters in the Lord. In the first reading we hear how God bestows the Spirit on seventy elders and how they began to speak out in His name. Two others who were not in the tent had also received the Spirit. Joshua was a bit disturbed. He asked Moses to put a stop to that. Moses was quick to point out that God bestows His gifts upon all of His creation. There is no need to feel jealous or envious. Wouldn't it be wonderful if more people were influenced by the Spirit?

In the Gospel reading, the disciples have a similar problem. They are driving out demons in your name Lord but they are not one with us. Who do they think they are? Those strangers should not be included in our special circle of friends. Jesus simply reminds them and us: "Anyone who is not against us is for us." In other words, He was saying only those who freely choose to reject the kingdom are not part of it.

It is sad to say but we can exclude ourselves as well as others from that kingdom by the example we give. It is what we say and do that really matters. If you and I do not live up to what we believe we could be in trouble. Who needs a millstone around their neck? If our hand, or foot or eye does not help us to bring about the kingdom then we fail to give good example of what we believe. Others suffer because of our lack of care and concern. Our eyes are to be open to the needs of those around us, especially those in our families who may be in trouble and are hurting. Our hands are to be extended in loving service of the kingdom. Our feet are to walk in the ways of the Lord bringing about unity, peace and love knowing Jesus as the way, the truth and the life.

Our second readings often tell us what we are to do as Christians. James has once again something wonderful to tell us. It is wisdom that is over and above the wisdom of this world. Don't be fascinated with money and what it can buy. There is no point having all kinds of clothes in your closet where the moths will have a feast day. Be careful what you store up for yourselves for those last days. See if all your wealth will bring you the happiness you long and search for. Be just and fair in all that you do. Look to the needs of others instead of always thinking about self. Selfish and greedy people have little faith and even less trust in a loving God who will provide not all that we desire but certainly all that we need each day of our lives. A large accumulation of money in the hands of the few is truly a scandal to all of God's poor. There are more than enough multi-millionaires in the news these days that live in luxury and will never be able to spend their wealth.

The values we live by tell the world who we are and what we believe. As God's people, brothers and sisters in the Lord, we are to live out our days by saving others and through that process bring salvation to ourselves. Now we know who they are. God bless.

27ᵗʰ OT B – Loneliness Sunday

Scripture: Genesis 2:18-24, Hebrews 2:9-11, Mark 10:2-16

It seems as though we are living in an age of loneliness. We struggle to avoid its pain and suffering and will go to any extreme to be rid of it. Loneliness is part of being human and is part of life's journey. It comes in many forms: failure, fear, separation and alienation, certainly death. It comes when we least expect it. We can be terribly lonely in a crowd, empty inside while having everything, cut off from each other by our modern world of TV screens and monitors. Loneliness makes us sad and we long to be one with one another. As creatures we long to be one with the Creator.

God knows our loneliness, our alienation and separation. He knows our need to love and to be loved in return. It is not good for anyone to be alone, to be without someone who cares. This is perhaps the reason why a man leaves his father and mother and clings to his wife.

The exchange between the Pharisees and the Lord has to deal with all human relationships and not just marriage itself. We know that the divorce rate has increased but a brief glance at the paper or the six o'clock news tells us about the further break down of family life. There is more child abuse, more spouse abuse, more teen age suicide, families and individuals that no longer speak to one another. We could spend hours trying to sort out why. But one thing is significant: When important relationships break down no one wins. There are no instant potions or pills, no easy solutions to this business of loving. It is real, honest, hard work, day in and day out that demands the very best in us.

What is more important? Our reverence, respect and love for one another or all the rules and regulations that allow for separation and divorce. The Scribes and Pharisees did not understand. God does not approve of stubbornness nor the pain and sorrow of divorce and broken families.

A sound, healthy marriage is a model of mutual respect and love which is essential in any relationship. Life by itself is not complete or enriching without a deep personal regard for another. No one is an island. No one is a rock. We need each other and we depend more and more upon each other with every passing day.

True friendship is an experience of self giving. It can be destroyed by a focus on my needs and my rights or it can be life giving when there is a patient, gentle dialogue that brings about solutions to problems. It can be one-sided when there is no appreciation of the other and expectations are unreal or it can be exciting and fulfilling when we listen and learn and try to understand someone different. It can be shallow and fragile when the hard times are ignored or pushed aside and not honestly shared instead of facing those tough decisions.

Whoever said that life must be free from loneliness, from pain and suffering or trial and tribulation? In fact such hardships need not be destructive. They can bring about a greater love for one another. We often read in the scriptures that Jesus was made perfect through His suffering. We know that suffering can open up our hearts to receive and to give love in return. Suffering and loneliness can strengthen our faith and bring us a promise of a new tomorrow.

As we come together to share in the one bread and the one cup, we celebrate the ideal of love. The Eucharist makes us one in mind and one in heart with others and the Lord. Through this marvelous exchange we find the courage and strength to be God's holy people.

God bless.

28th B – Riches Sunday

Scripture: Wisdom 7:7-11, Hebrews 4:12-13, Mark 10:17-30

All of us want to feel that we are in charge of our lives, that we have things under control. We long to be secure. We work hard to free ourselves from hunger, from the cold and from being poor. We work for what we get and we never seem to get ahead or to be satisfied. We would like to think that we have arrived but we are still on our way. It is sad to say that many people are driven more by their desires and wants than by the values Jesus has given us.

The story of the rich man seems to fit as well in our day as it did then. "What must I do to share in everlasting life?" Well, it isn't just a matter of fulfilling all the rules and regulations. No, that is not going to do it. There is more. It isn't just a loving look, a glance from the Lord that can make the difference or bring about changes, although that could happen. Jesus' words are always challenging. There is always more to be done. "Yes, go and sell what you have and give it to the poor." At this we read that the man's face fell. He went away sad because he could not let go of all that he had. The rich man thought he could find security in all his wealth, all that he owned. Maybe his wealth was a sign of God's favor!

The wisdom of our world, conventional wisdom as it is called, urges us to work on three guarantees for success. Marcus Borg called them: achievement, affluence, and appearance. What do we look for in life? Here is a list that fits: a good education, a well paid job, a new home, a new car, time away for an extended vacation. Of course, we need a good bank account with plenty of high grade stocks, and most of all we need to cultivate an image of never growing old, staying trim and neat so as to have a classy look.
The list could be endless. The more we have the more we want. Jesus is trying to tell the rich man and also us that things will never satisfy. The only security is in our God and in His kingdom of loving service.

We know there is nothing evil about having money. It is what we do with what we have that counts. It is a matter of attitude. So often those who have money and riches feel superior to those who do not. They see themselves as privileged, special, over and above and not as brothers and sisters with God's poor. In God's kingdom there cannot be and must not be first and second class members.

We are all God's people and we are to share what we have with those who are less fortunate. We are to live simply so others might simply live!

In order to do that we are to seek the wisdom that Jesus offers so that we know what we need rather than what we want or told we must have. To live simply is to know when we deprive others of their rightful share of all that God has provided for His people. To live simply is to give of our time, our talent and our treasure for the building of God's kingdom so that others are enriched by our care, concern and love.

It was a very sad day when the rich young man turned away from the Lord because he was unwilling to give up all that he had. It is also a sad day when you and I know that the riches offered by the Lord far exceed what we could ever have and yet we would rather not give up our pursuit of the so called "good life" offered by the world.

Then we read: Who then can be saved? Jesus then fixed His eyes on them and said: "For human beings it is impossible but with God all things are possible. You and I are to find our security only in God's love. God Bless

29th OT B – Service Sunday

Scripture: Isaiah 53:10-11, Hebrews 4:14-16, Mark 10:35-45

In our daily search for happiness we can sometimes lose our way. If only I could win the lottery. That might do it! Some might think that power or prestige of an elected office might make life worth living. Others would rather take the easy way out, just sit back and enjoy all the good things the world has to offer. Still others think they have all the answers. They are unwilling to try new ways to find the happiness they long for. It seems that all of us try often enough to take the easiest way out so as to avoid any pain or suffering in our search.

James and John thought they would find their happiness, their greatness sitting one at the right and one at the left of the Lord when He comes into His glory. They thought He would be the One to make Israel a great nation. "You do not know what you are asking," Jesus told them. Are you ready to pay the price? It is not going to be easy. The price of happiness will cost some suffering. Of course, they did not understand and neither did the others. Perhaps that is why they were so angry and envious. Jesus was going up to Jerusalem to die. They thought He was going there to become their Ruler. Those in high places of authority issued the orders and all the others carried out those orders or there would be hell to pay if they did not. They thought they could rule by force and fear and not by the love that Jesus would show them.

"No, it cannot be that way with you!" Jesus told them. Anyone who wants to be great must serve the rest. Whoever wants to rank first among you must serve the needs of all. We are to find our happiness in serving others and not ourselves and that is hard to understand. It is a paradox. St. Francis knew this well: "It is only in giving that we receive. It is only in pardoning that we are pardoned." It is in being empty of our selfish needs and desires that we can be filled with God's love. It is only in letting go that we are able to do God's will and offer ourselves in loving service.

First of all this loving service begins at home with one another who live under the same roof. It is listening and sharing, taking time for each other so that family life becomes the source of our security, strength and love. That means that parents must see their roles as fathers and mothers as the most important service of all. Their love for each other is to be reflected in their care, concern and love for their children. These days there seems to be a greater need for patience and forgiveness, understanding and compassion for those who strive to be family for each other.

Our loving service is also our job, our daily work which provides our daily bread. We are to use the gifts and talents we have received from our generous God to provide not only for ourselves but also for the good of others. We have responsibilities to our employers just as they have responsibilities to us. There must be a just day's labor for a just day's pay.

We also have responsibilities for our Church and our community. We are to share our time, talent and our treasure to bring about the kingdom: to teach our children, to foster and bring about their well-being through proper education. We also have a responsibility to improve the social and cultural environments of our town, to work together in harmony attracting new industry and business. That also means that we are responsible citizens paying our fair share of taxes for education, good government and city improvement. If we take time to look around our neighborhoods and town there is much to be done in order that our living here might be more fulfilling and enriching.

As Christians you and I are to find our greatness in serving the needs of others. Either we are on our way doing that or we are in the way not fulfilling our responsibilities. Take some time to think about this during this coming week and see what you can do. God Bless.

30th OT B – Bartameus Sunday

Scripture: Jeremiah 31:7-9, Hebrews 5:1-6, Mark 10:46-52

It must be difficult and extremely hard to live everyday in total darkness. Just think; never to see the beauty of creation, the first light of day or the colors of a beautiful sunset; never to enjoy the beauty of flowers and trees, streams and lakes; never to look into the face of someone you love or loves you in return; never to notice the smile and excitement in a child's eyes or the beauty etched in the face of someone who has grown old in loving others and doing good for them. How special is the gift of sight! How fortunate we are that we can see.

This evening we hear the story of the blind Bartameus and how Jesus opens his eyes. Jesus does more than give him sight. He also enlightens his mind and heart and gives him a new vision of what life can be. Bartameus jumps up, throws off his old, dirty, ragged coat (his old way of looking at life) and in his great need comes to be healed. "Master, I want to see." "Your faith has healed you." Immediately he received his sight and started to follow Jesus up the road.

Mark is trying to open up the eyes of all of us who choose to follow the Lord of Life. This miracle story follows the teachings we heard these past few weeks. First of all Jesus taught that marriage is sacred. Marriages are to reflect the love that God has for all of creation. Next, He taught that the meaning of life is much more than acquiring riches, getting ahead of others and it does not matter how you do it. Last week we heard that the Son of Man has come to serve and not to be served, to give His life in ransom for many. We are not to lord it over others but to give ourselves in loving service. All of these teachings were in opposition to what His disciples expected just as they are for us during these days. There are no short cuts, no easy way to follow the Lord. We need our eyes opened so that we might see what the kingdom of God is all about.

There is none so blind as those who choose not to see. Many see only what they want to see. There are some who prefer not to see what God would have them become. In a sense we are all blind in one way or another. To recognize our blindness is to admit of our shortcomings, our weaknesses and failings, our selfishness and sin. Like Bartameus we are to be people of faith asking the Lord to open our eyes so that we might see what is to be done.

Instead of being short sighted we are to notice those who are close to us and part of our lives each day. We are to notice all those who do good for us and the needs they might have. We are to become more aware of their love, their care and concern instead of being overcome with the darkness of doubt, discouragement and despair. We are to open our eyes to see the love the Father has bestowed upon us by giving us His Son to be our Savior and Lord.

Like Bartameus, people of faith we pray: Lord, that we might see the values of our faith and be drawn closer to you and to one another. Lord, that we might see the goodness in each person we meet and work with. Lord, that we might see our own special gifts and talents and use them to bring about your kingdom of love. Lord that I might see; that we all might see the beauty, the joy, the happiness that is ours if only we follow in the way of your Son.

Amen and God bless.

31st OT B – Love Sunday

Scripture: Deuteronomy 6:2-6, Hebrews 7:23-28, Mark 12:28b-34

Being very practical people and of course very human most of us like to take the easy way out. There is no sense in re-inventing "the wheel!" Maybe that is why we like laws, rules and regulations. They show us how to order our lives with the least amount of energy expended. They point out the way and help us make the right decision. If we fulfill the law then we have done what is expected or required. We are deserving of a reward or at least a pat on the back. Rules, regulations and laws help us to make the proper response to most of life's problems. At least, we think so!

The Scribe in the gospel story this evening wanted to be sure he made the right response. There were over six hundred rules and regulations in the law and he had to know which one of all these rules was the most important. Jesus, being a good Jew responded by quoting the Shema, a prayer memorized in early childhood: "Hear O Israel, the Lord our God is Lord alone! Therefore you shall love the Lord your God with all your heart, all your soul, all your mind and all your strength." Then Jesus added: "You shall love your neighbor as yourself. There is no other commandment greater than these."

"Ah! You are right teacher", he said. Love is the most important thing we do. And then Jesus went on to tell him: "You are not far from the kingdom of God." Apparently there was something lacking in his response. More had to be done. He needed to take that all important truth and put those loving words in action. When you say you love someone it is more than just words. That expression "I love you" demands some evidence, some positive indication that you truly care. Certainly it is important to tell others we love them but it is more important to show that we do. Many times it only becomes a nice phrase to be said with the hope of getting that love in return.

We cannot love our God without loving our neighbor. Nor can we love our neighbor without loving our God. In fact, we cannot love God or our neighbor unless we first love ourselves. Love is that binding force that keeps all of God's creation together and that is what the kingdom of God is all about.

Everyday we are challenged to live and love as Jesus did. First of all, if we are in love with God we will be people of prayer. We need to spend time with Lord not only in our need but in thanksgiving. Each and every day is a gift! We are to become more aware of His presence in the circumstances, events and people who are part of our lives. We do what God wants us to do not because of rules or regulations but because we are in love with this all loving God.

If we love our neighbor we will be more aware and truly appreciate their goodness, their care, concern and their love. We will be patient, understanding and forgiving of their faults recognizing our own humanness in them. We are to respect and love them because they too are loved by the very same love we have received from our God.

However, without a real and honest love for ourselves we cannot love God or our neighbor. We are to accept our humanness and that includes all of our faults and failings, even our sinfulness and know in faith God's merciful compassion and forgiveness. We are to embrace the shadow in our lives, that dark place we prefer not to visit. We are to realize that God has first loved us just as we are. Knowing that love, we are able to change and become that beautiful person God has called us to be.

Laws, rules and regulations just don't do it. We are to be lovers willing to put our lives on the line for the kingdom. With God's help we will make that kingdom of love a reality in our day. God Bless

32nd OT B – Widow Sunday

Scripture: 1 Kings 17:10-16, Hebrews 9:24-28, Mark 12:38-44

It may sound strange but the secret of our giving of our time, talent and our treasure is our willingness and readiness to receive. So often we feel that we can do things on our own, that we don't need others to help us through a particular dark and depressing time. We need to be strong; we tell ourselves and are independent people. It is that old American ideal of rugged individualism that I can pull things together by myself and work through whatever may happen. We don't need others and sometimes we feel that we don't need our God. Maybe that is why our Churches are so empty these days. Maybe people have become too self-sufficient.

The scriptures this evening remind us about our investments in life. I suppose this would be the ideal time to talk about money and giving to the Church. Perhaps that is something you should pray about but there is more. I think the scripture also talks about the gifts of time and talent and our trust in our God as we gratefully respond for all that has been given. It isn't the Scribes and Pharisees who get our attention. They want their special treatment because they have observed all the laws, rules and regulations. No it is the widow who handed over her last penny. She who gave so little really gave so much. She sacrifices all that she has while the wealthy give only of their surplus. Her sincere giving from her want is an ideal for all of us.

This ideal includes giving money but the meaning goes far beyond that. It is about giving but also trusting God with our very lives. It is again letting go and letting God be God for us. It is living generously each and every day relying not on ourselves but humbly depending upon our God who will take care of our every need. Needs have to do with the essentials of life but wants are forever!

It is the widow who is vulnerable, powerless and poor. She is the one who should be on the receiving end of things. Instead she freely gives of all that she has. She is another model of faith, a faith that is generous, and a faith that is trusting. She is willing to go away empty handed, living in hope and trusting what is to come. Like the widow in the first reading she knows that the jar of flour will never go empty nor the jug of oil go dry.

That kind of faith and trust is possible only when we appreciate God's gifts to us. Knowing God's generosity and His care for us we are then able to give of what we have received. Our faith tells us that God will return and restore what we have shared.

It is really a paradox, isn't it? The more we give of our lives, the more we receive, the more we experience life in its fullness. It is in this sharing of life with one another that we become the presence of God for those in need. Lest we forget, we are all needy in one way or another!

We find joy in giving and responding to the needs of others because we have also been needy. Others have been there for us, showing us the Lord's compassion, mercy, forgiveness and love. These people are a source of strength for us and renew our faith in God who will see us through the good times as well as the bad.

To be good givers, we must first learn how to receive. When we know what we have been given, we can easily share of who we are and what we have. Why? Because we are all one family, daughters and sons of a loving God. God Bless

33rd OT B – End Sunday

Scripture: Daniel 12:1-3, Hebrews 10:11-14, 18, Mark 13:24-32

We are coming to the end of the year, the end of the season, the end and the beginning of a new time in the Church year. All endings are frightening because we know we must begin something new. Trials, wars, violence, earthquakes and darkened days are always signs of an ending time. We know that one day the world will end and it does not matter what the end looks like or even when it will happen. We just know that life has a beginning, middle and an end. Our lives are novels we write while living each successive day. Our lives are journeys with succeeding stages. We have a goal, a purpose, a conclusion, a place to go but we do not have all the time in the world.

Our time is short. It is later than we think. The older we get the more we can appreciate and love life. With each passing day we get a little older and like good wine, a little better and hopefully a little wiser.

Our scriptures on this rather dark November evening speak to us about the end of time and the signs of the Lord's second coming. They are frightening signs but not signs that paralyze us with fear or cause us not to have hope. We are followers of the Lord of life and He has shown us how to overcome all suffering, doubt, despair and darkness, even death itself. He has shown us that suffering is not the final reality, that evil will never triumph over good, that death will never have its final say. As His sons and daughters we do not take His promises lightly. We are people of promise, people who hope and trust in the goodness, mercy and love of our God.

But just imagine if the world were to end now. Maybe next Wednesday or later on this evening! Maybe some good things have been done but there may be just a few more important things to do. I wonder about all that. In fact, I can think of three wonders.

First of all, if the world were ending, I would wonder if I had done the best I could to make this world a little better place for others and not just for myself. It would not have to be much because we can only give of what we have received. Have I added some goodness, some beauty, given some joy and peace, some love in my daily efforts to help others as I live out this mystery called life?

My second wonder is like the first, but I would wonder if I truly responded with love for those who so generously gave of their love for me. I think of my father and mother, my family and friends and all they did to bring me to this day. Did I just expect that they would always be there? Did I fail to recognize their humanness, their weaknesses and then blame them for all of my hardship, all my worries and difficulties in Life? I wonder if I have the love to be forgiving and able to let go of my angers and resentments for all those disappointments and hurts.

If the world were ending my final wonder is: Do I really believe in God? To live a life of faith is such a fragile, frightening and challenging way to go. It seems as though our faith is stronger some days than others and we wonder where God is. Did He abandon me? I think we all have our doubts, our discouraging and dark days. Maybe it is my problem; maybe it is because I expect God to fit into my little plan for life rather than do His will for my happiness and salvation.

We are all pilgrims, sojourners, on our way, still searching because we know in faith that there is more to life, that there is Someone in charge of it all and we know that Someone loves us. It is later than we think, but then thank God there is still time, time to work on all our wonders. Endings do bring new beginnings and our God is waiting for our response. God Bless.